THE
KING
OF
KINGS

TONI LALLUK

Hardcover: 978-1-963050-74-5
Paperback: 978-1-963050-20-2
eBook: 978-1-963050-21-9
Library of Congress Control Number: 2023922453

This Book is a work of non-fiction.

Unless otherwise indicated, Scriptures are taken from the New King James Version (NKJV). Copyright © 1982 by Thomas Nelson. Used by permission. All rights reserved.

Scriptures marked ESV are from the ESV ® Bible (The Holy Bible, English Standard Version®), copyright © 2001 by Crossway, a publishing ministry of Good News Publishers. Used by permission. All rights reserved."

Scriptures marked KJV are taken from the Holy Bible, King James Version (Authorized Version).

Scriptures marked NASB are taken from the NEW AMERICAN STANDARD BIBLE®, Copyright © 1960,1962,1963,1968,1971,1972,1973, 1975,1977,1995 by The Lockman Foundation. Used by permission.

Scriptures marked ASV are taken from the American Standard Version, which is in the public domain.

Capitalization has occasionally been modified from the original.

Ordering Information:

Prime Seven Media
518 Landmann St.
Tomah City, WI 54660

Printed in the United States of America

TABLE OF CONTENTS

Acknowledgement.. 1

Introduction 3

PART ONE: I am My Father's son. **17**

Chapter 1:   Like father, Like son 19
Chapter 2:   What is the gift of free will and
                why did God give it to humans?................... 28
Chapter 3:   Why did God create humans? 42

PART TWO: King Of Kings **53**

Chapter 4:   The fall of man 55
Chapter 5:   Kings of Israel 72
Chapter 6:   Medieval Kings 87
Chapter 7:   Modern Kings... 105
Chapter 8:   King Jesus 133

PART THREE: Conversations With My Father **173**

Chapter 9:   Start by listening 175
Chapter 10:   Communicate through prayer 196
Chapter 11:   Ask and receive 212
Chapter 12:   Watch out for signs.. 218
Chapter 13:   Obedience.. 226

PART FOUR: Our Father's Will.. **241**

Chapter 14:   Who is God?... 243
Chapter 15:   What is the real name of God? 259
Chapter 16:   The will of Jehovah 264

Synopsis 273

ACKNOWLEDGEMENT

This book was a long time in the making, even though I had to go through a personal transformation to get it started. However, there are people who have encouraged me to improve various aspects of my life. Because of them I have gracefully accepted to do things that inspire them. It is a simple thing to do when I consider that their joy and happiness means the world to me.

I want to thank Otis Lalluk for his ever-ready assistance when I run into trouble with my computer. You know a lot about the inner workings of my Lap-Top than I ever will. You are my go-to—IT Guy whenever I needed help.

Joya Lalluk, I do not have enough words to describe what you bring to the party, but sure enough everything lights up the moment you step into the room. You bring so much joy into our lives, and when the going gets tough you always find a way to help me take one more step. I love you, daughter.

To Linet Lalluk-Butijn; Thank you for your support and encouragement. You have always believed in me. Twenty-two years ago, you said to me; "You are going to be a writer." You have given your unconditional love and support every step of the way.

Finally, my sincere gratitude to the unknown lady who gave a lift to a stranger who looked totally different from her, from the port of Rotterdam to the central station. That was twenty-five years ago. I will never forget your kindness.

INTRODUCTION

After twenty years on the road, I have come to realize that long distance trucking can be compared to running a marathon. The wheels on the truck represent your legs, the constant hum of the engine is akin to your heartbeat distributing and circulating energy all over your body and your motivation is the amount you are paid after a successful delivery of the payload.

The journey is always full of twists and turns, and you are never certain where you'll stop to rest for the night.

I am a long-distance truck driver and on this trip my journey started the day before about 1600 kilometers away in Benicarlo on the eastern wings of Spain, with a night stop in between at a parking-lot in Clermont-Ferrand, France. Here I took the mandatory nine hours to rest and be ready to hit the road again the next day.

It was a warm day, with the temperature far above normal at 35 degrees centigrade, and it was so hot it looked as if the Sun was on steroids generating so much heat to punish the errant member of the solar system.

There was no wind and it felt as if the sweltering heat had conspired with a vapor-like haze in the atmosphere to give a sinister meaning to the word "Meltdown." I couldn't help but wonder how hell would be like if the earth could feel this way.

I had driven nine and a half hours when I arrived at the truck parking on the frontier between Belgium and the Netherlands. I parked my truck and switched on the stand-air conditioner. With the cool atmosphere in the cabin, I proceeded to do my paperwork when I heard a knock on the door. I looked out and saw an elderly lady with a friendly face standing beside the door. She smiled at me and asked; "Do you speak English?

I nodded, wondering how she could be smiling on a brutally scorching day like this. She said, "I know you are tired, but I'd like to give you something to read." She took from her bag a pamphlet with an illustration of a little girl holding a small plant in her hands and written boldly were the words; "HOW DO YOU VIEW THE FUTURE?

Just before she walked away over to the next truck, she said, "maybe you can read it in your spare time."

I have read this small material over and over, and I am somehow surprised that this small book is asking the very same questions that have been on my mind for a long time. Questions, why the conditions on earth keep deteriorating instead of improving. Questions, I keep hearing on my journeys to different places and in many cities where I have been to, while carrying out my duties as a transporter.

So, is there a voice hidden somewhere in your mind asking these questions:

What is wrong with the world?
What will our planet become?
What will the future look like?

I am sure you do. You are not the only one; In every village, every town and every city, all over the globe millions of people-both the haves and have not are asking these very same questions.

I am one of them; Because of the dangerous brew of disharmony and uncompromising-narrowmindedness in the world today, I am convinced that the ominous silence of previous and present mistakes will unleash a change that will shake the very foundations of the earth. That is why I am writing this book. I am acutely aware of the consequences of the deteriorating conditions of the environment:

- The rapid rate of adverse climate change globally.
- The rising cost of living.
- The burgeoning refugee crises and global hunger.
- Low morality and widespread corruption.
- Unnecessary wars, intolerance, discrimination and racism.
- The overwhelming scourge of bad leaders, bad rulers and bad governance.

With this on my mind, I would say that these are solvable issues that can be resolved by humans, therefore the persistence of these problems in our day-to-day reality is because our world is continuously debased by human errors and misplaced priorities-intentional and unintentional.

We know that these problems can be solved if rulers, leaders and those in power can mobilise their people in the best possible way, helping their societies to ensure the proper management of the environment and the appropriate utilisation of resources of their nations to provide sustainable development for its citizens.

Even though most of the problems facing the world today can be attributed to natural consequences of change in nature, modern globalization and unrestrained global economic growth, they are also the result of irrational management of natural resources, large-scale corruption and greed.

This is the reason why we have leaders or elect rulers all over the world: They are supposed to inspire, motivate and set good examples for people to accomplish positive changes in the world. Therefore, it would be correct to say that the inability to solve the myriads of problem in the world today can be traced to bad leadership.

The world is now saturated with bad leadership. You will find them in capitalist, democratic, communist, dictatorship, right-wing, left-wing, including rich and poor countries, and in all regions of the world. Because of this, it is easy to understand that there are no poor or third-world countries in the world—only bad leaders.

Their inability to lead and lack of direction stems from a leader's own lack of vision and over-rated leadership skills. Their sole motivation to rule stems from the selfish desire to acquire wealth and power and sustain this power through corruption. This has often resulted in rulers leading humanity to inflict unspeakable destruction, cruelty and suffering upon itself. Surely this is the direction the world is heading to.

However, it looks as if the situation of things in the world will steadily continue to go south in this particular way and it can no longer be reversed or changed by human efforts, nonetheless there are helpful steps everyone can take to make this bumpy ride of life on earth more meaningful and less cumbersome.

On that note, I would like to invite you to travel with me on this journey to find out how good governance, renewed nature and a better life are a real possibility for billions of people in a not-too-distant future.

But, before we proceed, it would be wise to underline the following issues:

- Why do we tolerate bad leaders and rulers?
- Why are we inclined to be governed by those who appear initially as heroes but soon slide into bad governance and corruption?
- Why are we willing to turn a blind eye to their misbehavior, and follow them unquestionably most of the time and even allow them to corrupt others?

These are the questions we ought to be asking ourselves.

For this reason, it is my personal wish to know, and to understand how everyone, both those who have and those that do not have, can achieve a meaningful, happy, and prosperous life, which is their God-given and divine right just like everyone else, without distinction.

Nevertheless, I am convinced we can find a way out of the numerous problems and corruption that surround us. Surely there's a way out. I believe this is not all there is for humanity.

I must confess that I faced existential challenges while growing up and survived a brutal civil war and unnecessary suffering caused by bad leadership. I was lucky not to be a statistic, and I was confronted at every level with man-made roadblocks of this worldly system of things.

These are the reasons that prompted me to start looking for answers in the Bible. Moreover, I remember a quote attributed to Albert Einstein, that "no problem can be solved from the same level of consciousness that created it."

I remember as a young boy growing up. I observed that my father had a peculiar habit of beginning his prayers with the words, "My Heavenly Father, Jehovah." It was his custom to pray with his family before every meal, in the mornings, and in the evenings before retiring for the day. And he always prayed in this manner, no matter the circumstances, for as long as I can remember.

Even then, I kept wondering if my father was fatherless, as I never knew my grandfather and my dad never spoke about his papa. So, one day I asked him, "Papa, why do you always begin your prayers with 'My Heavenly Father, Jehovah,' and why do you call Him Jehovah instead of God?"

My father looked at me, and with a bit of sadness in his voice, he said, "My father died when I was a young boy. I never got to know him, as I was raised by my mother and grandmother. So, I claimed God as my father, but when I learned that God's real name is Jehovah, I felt the right thing to do was to address Him by His real name."

He told me that his belief in God protected him and helped him to overcome many difficult situations. Therefore, he wanted me to adopt this belief and make it my way of life. Regardless of how much he tried, I was young, and I found it difficult to pray always. I was even skeptical as to whether this attitude that God will provide solutions to all my problems would really work out for me. So, I did things my own way, and on several occasions the decisions I made didn't work out well for me.

My father died many years ago, but I can still recall the last words he said to me. He said, "I am your earthly father. You and your brothers and sisters were given to me and your mother to love and mentor, to teach and protect and to guide you to become responsible human beings. But my time has come to say goodbye. I would advise that you look for your real Father when I am gone. Seek Him out and develop a relationship with Him, and He will teach and guide you much more than I was able to do."

Lastly, he said, "Promise me you will, and if you don't know how to find Him, you can use the Bible I gave to you, because the Bible will guide you straight to your real Father." And I promised him that I would.

Many years have passed, and I did not live up to my promise to my late father. I was impatient and stubborn, and I believed in this worldly system of things. I made many mistakes. But after years of moving, drifting, stumbling, and growing, I remembered the promise I had made to my dad.

I still had the old Bible my father gave to me, so I began to look for answers in the Bible. In the beginning, I was just curious, but after a while, I noticed that I was gaining more knowledge and insight. Gradually, I could feel that I was changing from the inside out.

Reading the Bible regularly helped me to develop discipline to do what is necessary and resist the urge to do what is convenient. This way, I began to acquire knowledge through reasoning, and I began slowly to apply what I was learning to my behavior. After that, I began to learn about prayer, but I had to convince myself that if I drew close to God, He would draw close to me—a truth I read in the Bible.[1]

I knew that I would have to make the first move because I wanted to find out whether, if I asked to know God, He would be there already waiting for me in accordance with my prayers. In fact, I really wanted to know if He listened at all to prayers.

Therefore, my first move was to find evidence that I am really the son of God and not only the son of my father and mother—or some creature of evolution that was shaped, formed, and controlled by the environment or the continent where I was born.

I really wanted to find out why my late father wanted me to seek for God. It was very important that I put this confusion to rest because the teachings of the Church and the school I attended were at loggerheads regarding the origins of humans.

With knowledge from the Bible, especially from the book of Genesis, I understood that I was made in the image and likeness of God, and He is the Creator, or the real Father, of all humans. He is material and organized intelligence, possessing both body and spiritual awareness beyond form, time, and space. The Scriptures proved to me that God is the real Father my earthly father wanted me to seek.

I became convinced I had found Him because I noticed I was paying less attention to man-made conditions that used to irritate and bother me endlessly. Rather, my focus was more on how to improve myself by using the information I was gleaning from the Bible. Therefore, my budding faith and belief that I'd found Him opened the door to the

---

[1]   James 4:8.

relationship I have with Him to this day, because even in my thoughts, every prayer has been made manifest in my life just because I believed that God will answer any of my supplication without fail.

Looking back now on the process I went through to obtain this knowledge, I would say that when you have faith and belief that God will grant what you wish for without fail, then requesting it is not necessary. Instead, all you need to do is to send a prayer of thanksgiving for what you want in advance, prior to receiving it.

I have also realized that God is standing by to help you if you use the free will, He gave you to think and act in accordance with His way and purpose for all things. This includes your understanding that He has created you in His image and provided the laws, the forces, and the environment for you to create your reality. Therefore, believe and act in faith that all of these are working for you, and they will without fail, because God created the process of originating something from nothing, which is perfect for all creation, including yours.

I am very grateful that I have picked up this knowledge from the Bible, and I am not going to let it slip out of my hands. I am fully convinced that my relationship with God keeps getting better and better. I know that God will fully supply all my needs according to His riches in glory, both material and spiritual. I remain ever grateful for the day I made the decision to start reading the Bible, because it has changed my life tremendously for the better.

I am therefore obliged to write this book to explain the process of using the information readily available in the Bible to anyone in their quest for a better way of living, even in the midst of a corrupt and problematic world. It is my sincere hope that the information they will obtain from reading this book will change their lives as well.

For this purpose, I testify that "all Scripture is inspired by God and beneficial for teaching, for rebuke, for correction, for training in righteousness."[2] The Bible will help you to realize what is wrong in your life. It will also correct you and help you to learn to do what is right.

From my personal experience, I would say that information from the Bible will help you to see the true plight of humans in order to understand why there is so much unhappiness in the world and how you can create happiness for yourself and those around you.

The Scriptures will help you to come to the understanding that there can never be a human solution to the problems caused by human rulership. It will present you with evidence that proves from the origins of creation that humans were not created to rule themselves or rule over another—rather, we are made to be ruled by God to fulfill our role as caretakers of the earth and other creatures.

I would recommend that you begin to use the Bible to find solutions to all your problems. The Bible will show you different ways to extricate yourself from the gripping tentacles of unwise and unhealthy habits that want to hold you down. It will guide you to find a safe path through the minefield of this complicated world system.

The Bible is also one of the most affordable books in any bookshop, and sometimes you may obtain it for free. Moreover, it is translated into almost every language, and it is available in most parts of the globe.

---

2   Second Timothy 3:16 NASB.

Based mostly on information readily available in the Bible, I have divided this book into four parts. The four parts are related to general information from the present system of things found in any part of the globe where you live at this point in time, from my own personal experience and from the Bible. You will see how I applied this knowledge to find peace of mind and success. I hope it will help you in the same way.

PART ONE: I AM MY FATHER'S SON

You will find evidence that God is the Father of everyone, and because He is, He has a duty and obligation toward His children, and we have a duty toward Him as well. If you decide to seek Him, you'll learn how you can find Him. Or if your relationship with Him is broken, you can use the same guidelines to rebuild it. In this part of the book, God's unique gift to His children is explained, as well as how you can use this gift to attain and achieve your chosen goal or conquer any obstacle you may encounter.

The Bible explains why God created humans. I know many people would really like to know why God created us and why He placed us on planet earth—I know because I used to ask these questions myself. But through correct understanding of the Scriptures, you will understand why He made us and what our responsibilities are for this unique gift of life that He gave us.

PART TWO: KING OF KINGS

It would be wrong to assume that God does not care about all that is going on all over the earth or that He is not concerned or aware of the difficulties and problems His children are going through due to mismanagement and misrule by their leaders. He knows He created a beautiful world, and He placed humans in charge to take care of it and understands that it will continue to be beautiful if we stop doing bad things to it and follow His original plan. This can only be realized if we decide to do the right things by righteously using the free will, He gave to us.

It is not God's fault that we humans choose the wrong options by deciding to do things our own way. Our choices are the cause of untold hardship for millions of people today. But the Bible has revealed to mankind that God will not allow things to continue to deteriorate in this way forever to the extent that it becomes irreversible.

God is merciful, and because of His unconditional love for humans, He sent His first Son, who lives in heaven with Him, down to the earth to make things right and show us the way and bring to us the good news of how He is going to fix all that has gone wrong with the world. This Son of God is the King of kings, and the Bible will help you to understand how great He is, how wealthy He is, and how powerful He truly is, as well as all the other attributes that elevate Him beyond any king that ever lived.

This part of the book describes how you can seek God through Jesus for truth and knowledge to live and succeed in this universe that He specially designed and created for all of us. You will also learn how individuals in the past and present with barely enough resources to meet their basic needs became wealthy, powerful, and successful. You will get the necessary experience and a massive dose of inspirational reality to overcome any problem. In short, you will understand that you don't have to face your situation alone because you are beloved and protected by the greatest King of all.

PART THREE: CONVERSATIONS WITH MY FATHER

Many people might have concluded it is not possible to have a conversation with God or even to communicate with Him. But they don't know how wrong they are. Certainly, it is possible to communicate with God and have a conversation with Him, only it may not be in our human way of thinking. You will learn how to approach God, how to listen, and how you can understand that He is the One speaking to you, because God our Father is ever ready to answer His children's smallest or greatest supplication.

God is actually expecting you to ask so you can develop your intuitive mind to hear Him loud and clear, like countless others before you. He will strip away your awkwardness and hesitancy to make you bold to understand that He sees only your divine self, which He created perfect in His own image and likeness—both spiritual and physical—and He will choose either of these channels to communicate with you.

PART FOUR: OUR FATHER'S WILL

The last part of this book helps you to develop a real sense of why you are here on earth and God's purpose for you. You will find out why and how you can serve and worship Him and why you should have a strong faith based on a deep understanding that He wants you to thrive and prosper. He also wants you to love and care for others and to use your awesome intelligence to care for nature, the environment, the animals, and other creatures that share this universe with us.

Further, in Part Four, you will find out through the Bible our Creator's real name. God our Father has many names and titles, and

His children all over the world have diverse and different names for Him according to their language and region of the world where they live.

How we call Him plays no role in His love for us. He is not greatly offended by our various names for Him because it is our nature as humans to develop fondness and affinity through names, as this comes along with the free will He gave to us. At the same time, God has a name, and just like us, He prefers to be called by His real name. Because of this, He told us His real name and where to find it. Once you realize how powerful this name is, you'll always address Him by His real name, especially when you find out that there is nothing too big or even impossible to accomplish for one who knows the power of God's name and His Word and chooses to call upon his Father in this way. For, by this name, he or she unleashes an action of unseen forces that can rebuild his or her body and repair his or her affairs.

If you know the will of God and His real name, you will learn to let go and let Him do and perform His will for you, which may appear as a miracle to you, but this is truly His will manifested and materializing into physical results.

Finally, I have written this book with the sincere intention that you will direct your attention to the one and only true source from which our life force flows. It will help you to wise up to the art of living with joy and the knowledge to accomplish your most cherished dreams.

It is therefore my prayer that you will enjoy every step of your journey into a satisfying future, of a truly fulfilling new way of living.

TONI LALLUK

PART ONE:

I AM MY FATHER'S SON

CHAPTER ONE

LIKE FATHER, LIKE SON

So God created man in His own image;

in the image of God He created him;

male and female He created them. (Genesis 1:27)

I have always found it disturbing to suppose that humans evolved from apes, and all through my adolescent life I looked for ways to reconcile the teachings of the Church and the schools on this subject. But no matter how I tried, I only succeeded in creating more confusion in my mind regarding this important issue.

Because of this, I was eager to find out how humans came to be here on earth and who our real Father and Creator is. I also wanted to know if we really look like Him and what His purpose was for creating us. However, as there is no schoolbook on biology or history that provides incontrovertible proof on this issue, I decided to seek the Bible's viewpoint. I affirm that with information from the Bible, I have found the answers to my questions regarding the origins of humans.

If you are looking for answers on how to find the true genealogy of mankind or how to find God, it would be wise to start your search with the Bible because it is the only archive containing correct information and the historical evidence of human origins.

I know who my real Father is. I know God is my Father because He said so in the Bible, which I regard as the best book of knowledge. In His own words, He made it very clear beyond reasonable doubt that I am a formal, visible, and understandable physical representation of who He is, and I am endowed with His attributes. To prove this, He made me in His own image and according to His own likeness.

This means He intentionally created me with the ability to communicate both spiritually and physically and to systematically use words, symbols, and body gestures, in combination with postures and facial expressions, for the following purposes:

- To become an individual who can use his free will to make my life what I want it to be in the future.
- To think about myself, others, and life in general and to ponder the past, present, and future, as a trait inherited from and befitting the nature of my Creator.
- To be unique and one of a kind in my individual DNA and yet to inherit genes, traits, and behaviors from my parents, uncles, aunts, grandparents, and great grandparents, with the ability to pass on to the next generation God's patent design and purpose of making another one of a kind.

- To be special in my own way, with preferences, gift and talents, perspectives of likes and dislikes, combined with color to make me exceptional and beautiful to behold as a member of my species.

For these important reasons, He created you and me to be human—in order to differentiate us from all the other creatures that He made. He also chose to reveal His nature, His thoughts, and His personality to us. He made Himself known because He wants His sons and daughters to have a personal relationship with Him so we can truly get to know Him intimately.

That is why He said in Isaiah 54:10, "'For the mountains shall depart and the hills be removed, but My kindness shall not depart from you, nor shall My covenant of peace be removed,' says the LORD, who has mercy on you."

Further, He declared; "When you pass through the waters, I will be with you; and through the rivers, they shall not overflow you. When you walk through the fire, you shall not be burned, nor shall the flame scorch you," says God in Isaiah 43:2, emphasizing how precious we are to Him.

When I read this from the Bible, I realized how valuable all humans are to God our Father and how blessed we are to be endowed with a complete package of creative engineering, containing all the aspects of His personality. It is humbling to find out that all human beings are specially crafted to consist of body, mind, and spirit. We are distinctly created to be spiritual beings living in a physical body.

To ensure that His children make perfect use of this awesome nature of what we are, God bestowed on us a phenomenal hard drive known as free will so that we can use it to choose what we want and to make the right decisions, as the case may arise.

HOW TO FIND GOD

Our first earthly father, Adam, was disobedient and sinned against God. Therefore, we became separated from God, and our perfect image before God became tarnished. This unclean spot from Adam has ensured that we have all done, thought, or said bad or sinful things at one time or another.

The result is that we are now spiritually separated from God. So long as one remains in this condition, it is impossible to have a relationship with God. But this does not mean that God does not love us. Rather, He made a provision that makes it possible for us to have a relationship with Him or heal a broken relationship with Him. God sent His Perfect Son, Jesus, to be born and raised on earth to show us the way to rekindle our lost relationship with Him.

In John 3:16, the Bible says, "God so loved the world that He gave His only begotten Son [Jesus Christ], that whoever believes in Him should not perish but have everlasting life." Remarkably, Jesus was not sent to judge us, but He came for our sins to be forgiven and for us to be saved through Him.

He demonstrated this love for us by dying on the cross in order to make this possible. But Jesus rose from death and went to heaven, and He still lives there with our Heavenly Father, preparing and waiting for the appointed time to deliver the final salvation.

You can get to know God by attending the meetings of any church or any Christian event or gatherings in your area. By going to meetings in any Christian church, you'll receive guidelines and help on how to connect with God. However, I would caution that the church is like a GPS navigational instrument. Though you can switch it on at the start of your journey and it will point the direction for you, the actual driving must be done by you. So, if you are seeking to have a relationship with God, you can start by thanking Jesus for His sacrifice on your behalf, bearing in mind His very own words: "I am the way, the truth, and the life. No one comes to the Father except through Me."

Make up your mind and use your heart to draw close to God by praying with an honest heart, and you will notice a good and calm feeling inside of you. This is because the channel is now open for communication between you and God, and His attention is now available to you.

Your relationship with God is much like two people associating with each other, who can only keep their close relationship going by being open with each other and communicating more when they encounter issues and by understanding and respecting each other.

When you pray, put your heart into it, because prayer is the channel through which we communicate with our Father. By this, your mind is better able to become quiet before God, to contemplate His Word and to seek His will for you. If your mind is not quiet while you are praying, your prayer is just words and mostly meaningless, and in this way you treat God perfunctorily, saying a few random words. Make sure you are not just reciting words by heart like empty religious rituals, clinging to rules that do not open your heart to God or help you seek His will.

You do not show respect for God when you say prayers without really meaning what you are saying, because this kind of prayer pertains only to outward appearance and religious ritual, and there is no real interaction with your Father in the Spirit. Therefore, prayers like this are not heard by God, and it becomes difficult for you to feel the presence of God, thereby making your relationship with Him more distant.

"God is Spirit, and those who worship Him must worship in spirit and truth."[3] When you pray to our Father, you must speak sincerely and truthfully. You must bring your real situation, difficulties, hardship, and of course your joy before Him and tell Him about them. Then ask for His will and the path to practice His will, for only this way will your prayers conform to God's plans for you.

HOW YOU CAN REBUILD YOUR RELATIONSHIP WITH HIM

Perhaps you have rebelled against God, and you feel your relationship with Him is broken. Or, you encounter some difficulties in life, and you see yourself living in a situation where you are constantly sinning and being tormented by these sins. Perhaps now you realize how much you have drifted away from God, and you wish to repent and reestablish your relationship with Him.

Now you must open your heart and tell Him about these problems and your desire to repent of your mistakes. Then you must ask for

---

[3]   John 4:24.

forgiveness and show your sincere wish to seek His will by asking for guidance. When you open up to God like this from the bottom of your heart, your heart is truly grieved to see how much you have rebelled and the consequences of your rebellion.

At this time of repentance, you'll notice your relationship with God getting better and better, and you'll feel that you're really close to Him again, as though you can feel His presence around you. This is the result of sincerely opening your heart to Him.

It is good to note that opening you heart to God has nothing to do with how much you say to Him or whether you use flamboyant words and lavish praises on God. Rather, it means telling Him about the true state of things with you, silently or with words, and seeking clarity and guidance from Him.

In this condition, whether you are at devotional gatherings or alone walking down the street, your heart will always remain silently open to Him in prayer without your being aware of it. Now you have inner peace, and you become quieter and calmer before God than you were at the beginning.

At this stage, you'll feel that your relationship with God is extremely close, as if you were face to face with Him, to the extent that you will understand more of His will. Now, when you encounter issues in life or with other people, you'll know how to practice truth and love to satisfy God with the wisdom to make the right decision. In this way, your relationship with your Heavenly Father becomes a normal part of your life.

In order not to relapse in your newfound relationship with God, it is important to practice spiritual devotions or activities, like daily

Bible reading and meditation on the words of the Bible. It is also good to ponder why God says such things as He does in the Bible, and what He wants to achieve by saying them. Moreover, you'll realize that God is honest, and He wants you to become an honest person.

You'll find out that God is faithful, and that there is no falsehood or deception in anything God says or does. He expects the same from us. It is therefore crucial that when you encounter issues in life, you remember your relationship with God and act in accordance with His Word.

Because of the special value of your relationship with God, remember not to rely on your own experiences or employ only human means to handle your problems, as most people do. Rather, seek His help to solve your issues and you will receive it. By doing this, your attitude will serve as a testimony to the purpose and will of God.

YOU CAN FIND GOD WITHOUT RELIGION

There are many people around the world who are seeking to find God on their own, because of their skepticism about religions of the world and how religions seek to draw adherents. Some of these people claim to be "spiritual but not religious," while some have no spiritual, religious, or scientific affinity to any source, power, or entity. Yet, due to personal reasons, private curiosity, or just the simple fact that they have been hurt or deceived by a faith community in the past, they now want to avoid religion as a means to find God.

Through ages and past civilizations, people have always had a sense of right—a belief that there is an absolute truth, order, and justice—that there must be One who is absolutely just, absolutely righteous, and absolutely perfect. In short, they have always believed that such a Being is out there, and they have sought to know Him.

Therefore, most people commonly believe that this Being is the greatest entity that they can conceive of—beyond all other things. They also agree that He is all knowing, absolutely powerful, and beyond space and time. The only Being that has these characteristics is God.

But there are many gods all over the world, so before you start looking for God, make sure you know who and what God is. You might need religion to find the true God. This does not mean you have to belong to any particular religious group. Rather, it means you have to use a religious tool like the Church or the Bible to help you find the One you are looking for.

The Bible is helpful because it gives you the direction and faith to know that the minute you start asking God to reveal Himself to you—with or without religion—you are truly on your way to finding Him. This is because God does not need religion to reveal Himself to you. But you will need the Bible to understand God's creative process and to see the written evidence that you are created by Him. The Bible is the first step.

If you are open-minded, you'll realize that science has already proven that there is an infinite intelligence behind all you see. Nature and the Bible reveal the Creator and the origin of all creation and the universe. Therefore, if you want to find God without religion, you already have. But if what you are searching for is something other than that…then that isn't God.

CHAPTER TWO

WHAT IS THE GIFT OF FREE WILL, AND WHY DID GOD GIVE IT TO HUMANS?

When God created humans, He gave them something unique among all other creatures that He had created. He gave us free will—the autonomy to make our own choices.

He designed and installed this "hard drive" inside humans to use, to choose, and to control the decisions we make. This free will is not something that acts independently from the human mind, but rather it acts in conjunction with the mind. It works in tandem such that whatever the mind deems desirable, the will is inclined to choose.

This means that our free will always acts according to the strongest inclination that we have at the moment of choice. When we have one, two, or many choices to make, our free will is automatically activated. But at the moment of choice, we'll certainly follow our strongest disposition, our strongest inclination, and our strongest desire, and this becomes our choice.

We also might make choices because we have no options. In this case, desire has nothing to do with our choice. For example, you are tired and there's a chair before you, so you choose to sit down because you're too weak to stand.

Sometimes we choose to do things that we really didn't want to do, because of coercion. This involves an external force that comes into our life that forces us to do things that under normal circumstances we would choose not to do. The power of coercion can severely hinder our freedom to make our own choices.

At other times, we may be forced into choices that are not directed by our own free will. This is often the case in society, where we have the knowledge that we must make our choices based on indoctrinated rules of where we are or where we live.

In this case, our inclination to choose is not determined by our personal self-determination but by the ideological consensus of where we are or where we live. This is a form of denial of freedom, because we cannot choose according to the strongest inclination of the moment that is ours but rather, we must defer to the dictates of the culture. Sometimes this is a good, civilizing force, and other times it is constraining in a way that denies essential freedoms.

Bear in mind that our desires determine our choices, and our choices must be free. Therefore, the essence of free will is to be able to determine what we want. If we do not have the freedom to choose, then our freedom is denied, because the self being able to determine its own choices is what free will is all about.

WHY DID GOD GIVE US FREE WILL?

God gave humans free will to dignify them and to differentiate them from all other creation. He made us in His image, unlike animals that act mainly on instincts. Humans have the capacity to display such qualities as love and justice like our Creator and the ability to know right and wrong.

Giving free will to us shows how much God loves us and how much He respects us. The Bible teaches us that God is almighty and His power is not limited by anyone other than Himself. Yet, He does not use this power to control everything that He created.

He also gave us free will because He wants us to be able to choose and to be responsible for the choices we make with the abilities He gave us. Having created us in His image, He wants us to make full use of the enormous capabilities that we have in our nature. He demonstrated His trust in us by giving us a free hand to use our natural and moral abilities.

NATURAL ABILITY

As humans, we have the ability to think and to imagine because it is in our nature to function in this way.

We have a natural ability to speak, to be kind and perceptive, and to make things happen with the world that we interact with.

We have the unique ability to walk upright.

We also have the ability to love and to hate and the ability to show emotion.

MORAL ABILITY

Human beings have the ability to be righteous, to know right from wrong, and to be in a state of justifiable freedom from sin or guilt.

We also have the ability to be sinful, to willingly choose to do wrong, and to be disobedient to God. We have the ability to be wicked and immoral.

Our natural ability is derived from the physical aspects of humans that refer to the human body, while our moral ability operates mainly with the spiritual aspect of humans. Therefore, to enable humans to make full use of our natural ability and our moral ability, God gave us free will.

Humans are also capable of acting spontaneously. Sometimes, we use our natural ability to carry out wrong moral decisions. However, there is no excuse for that because our free will is not just for making choices but for distinguishing between right and wrong and considering the consequences that may arise because of the choices we make. We please God by using our free will to worship Him.

HOW TO USE YOUR FREE WILL
TO ACHIEVE YOUR GOALS?

I must reiterate once again for clarity that free will is the perfect gift from God to humans to live a fulfilling, harmonious life. You must decide what you want to achieve and commit to it. Bear in mind that there may be plenty of prosperity and abundance on your path, but it can only be brought into manifestation through desire and through God's help.

Here are certain steps I suggest you follow:

1. DECIDE WHAT YOU WANT. All riches and all achievement begin to occur in the form of thought and lead you to choose what you desire most. Choose what is clearly understood by all aspects of your conscious and unconscious minds, because desire is the starting point of all achievements. So, ask yourself the following questions:

    > How can I draw nearer to God?
    >
    > What do I wish to accomplish?
    >
    > How much money do I want?
    >
    > What excites me in life?
    >
    > How do I want my future to look like?
    >
    > What type of people do I want to hang out with, etc.?

2. WRITE IT DOWN ON PAPER. Now that you have made up your mind what you want, the next step is to write it down on paper.

As you formulate your goals, be specific, and name the time limit you expect to meet certain measurable milestones. State what sacrifices you are willing to make in return and describe your plan of how you intend to achieve your goal.

This will force you to be definite and clear about your desire, and it will make this desire stick in your mind and trigger your brain to work on the details of making it happen. Make sure to aim high enough to really fire up your emotions. Indulge yourself by making your goal big and beautiful.

Write down a timeframe or date by which you wish to achieve this goal. Be aware that now that you have written it down, it becomes a commitment for you, and you have just set the wheels in motion.

Find a quiet place to be alone and read aloud or speak out what you want. Ask God for it. You can do this through prayer or speaking aloud. This means you are serious about it, for it is written and spoken. You have made the first move.

In the Scriptures, it is written: "Ask, and it will be given to you; seek, and you will find; knock, and it will be opened to you" (Matthew7:7).

By writing your desires down, asking God in prayer, and having faith that you will receive all that you ask for, you have now engaged the law of asking and receiving that triggers the miraculous manifestation power that fuels this law. You have stepped out in faith to receive what you seek.

3. HAVE AN ACTION PLAN. This will be the road map to follow that will guide you to your goal. Break it down into bite-sized chunks, identifying the task you have to do first to get the ball rolling. Consider if there are certain steps to prioritize or if there are time-sensitive tasks that you must do in a certain order and be clear about what you want to accomplish each step of the way.

By doing this, your goal will seem less daunting and more attainable. Your mind will start coming up with ideas, along with opportunities and people who can make your dream a reality. Sometimes, you may not get all the answers right away on the "how," but be patient. They will come to you at the right time.

Be flexible and ready to make necessary adjustments. This does not mean you have to abandon your plans if you hit a roadblock or traffic jam. Rather, it means you have to make a detour because there's a better way that will lead you to your goals. Use the opportunity to analyze your journey so far, and then readjust your plan and goal accordingly. God uses these detours and traffic jams to lead and teach and grow you, that you may mature in tandem with your goals.

No matter what happens or how long it takes, never ever give up on your goals and your dreams, because they are meant to come true. Sometimes, due to the adjustments you are forced to make, it might take a little bit longer, and what you achieve will be even bigger than what you imagined.

Focus on the reason why you must succeed. Remember, it is never too late, because no matter at what age you begin, or what happens, you can be successful.

4. TAKE ACTION. Now that you've written out your goals and a definite plan to carry them out, begin at once to put this plan in motion. It may seem scary to take that first leap, but you've got to start somewhere, and there's no better time than the present. So, dig deep and find your courage, and you'll start figuring it out as you go along.

Taking action also helps you to develop discipline to push forward, no matter the challenges that lie ahead. It will serve as a constant reminder that through your actions and your faith, your life is now in God's hands, and He will help you to become the kind of person you have chosen to be. Moreover, taking action keeps you sharp and awake to realize that everything that comes your way is an opportunity.

5. USE YOUR TALENTS AND EXPERTISE. By now, you must have recognized that everyone does something better than you— and likewise, you do something better than every person you meet. Therefore, when you start taking action to carry out your plans, it would be wise to think about what it will take to accomplish each task that makes up your main goal. This you will do by knowing your own strengths and weaknesses.

Everyone has a gift from God, and some people have skills and expertise necessary to accomplish what they set out to achieve. Now is the time to use this knowledge to motivate yourself by realizing that you don't want to stay where you are—you have a goal to reach.

Find out what your strengths are, accept them, and use them to launch yourself to where you want to be. You already have everything you need, only you don't know it yet. Be true to yourself by making the best use of what you have in your mind, your unique talents, and your God-given abilities.

6. HAVE A SUCCESS MINDSET. There is a power within you that is far superior to any condition or circumstance outside of you. This is the Spirit of God in you, a spiritual presence that you have inherited from God. With your free will you can control your thoughts to direct this power to achieve whatever results you choose, with the understanding that no experience you go

through—even trials—is wasted. Therefore, there is no failure. You are assured of success with God at your side.

This means continuously moving in the right direction toward your goal, believing that God will provide the abilities you need to do whatever it takes to succeed. With a success mindset, you have now reinforced your determination with an ironclad armor to support your conviction that "all things are possible to him who believes." Put your focus now on how to do it rather than on why you can't do it.

With the adoption of this mindset, you are firmly determined to discard any influence of unfortunate occurrences of the past and unfortunate or unfriendly environments of the present, knowing that you have the mental and physical ability to achieve your purpose in life. Now you can expect possibilities, because for you, there are no impossible dreams.

7. FAITH. You can be, you can do, and you can have anything that you want if you believe and have faith that you can. Faith is very crucial to success, and that is why in the Bible, faith is described as the substance of things hoped for and the evidence of things not seen.

Because of my strong belief in the Bible, I want to stress that it is very important that you have absolute faith that what you ask from God is what you will receive. Even Jesus demonstrated this when He said in Mark 9:23, "If you can believe, all things are possible to him who believes."

I would say that people who have achieved great things in life have succeeded because they had great faith in their God-given ability. It

is now time to stop worrying--time to have faith and create the space
to receive. You have to trust that it's done—it is already yours. In the
Bible, it is written in Mark 11:24: "Therefore I say to you, whatever
things you ask when you pray, believe that you receive them, and you
will have them."

The point the Bible is impressing upon you is that God is the great
unseen Provider who will go to work on your behalf in His own perfect
way to deliver what you have prayed for.

Some two thousand years ago, Jesus tried to explain to the masses
how important it is to have faith in God. He showed through action
and spoken word that He did all His great works and miracles because
He believed that whatever He asked from His Father, God would grant
His wish. Even if it means that He had to endure great suffering. But
speaking of the greatness of the works the Father will bless, Jesus
assured us that "he who believes in Me, the works that I do he will do
also; and greater works than these he will do."[4] I would suggest that
you believe Him and be willing to go where He leads you.

I know that in the twenty-first-century world of today, it is
sometimes very difficult to have faith. We are bombarded by so many
options, opinions, and distraction from news and social media that
deprive us of the ability to concentrate and have faith in ourselves and
faith in the infinite promises of God. In fact, many have come to accept
the popular notion that seeing is believing. It's too bad they do not
understand how wrong it is to harbor such a belief. Those who follow
God believe in things they do not yet see.

---

[4] John 14:12.

However, it is wise to bear in mind that we can receive God's blessings by taking the steps of faith that prepare our hearts to receive, because no one is ready to receive anything until he or she believes they can receive. Therefore, it is imperative that your state of mind be that of belief and not of mere hope or wishful thinking.

So, if you are having problems believing, or you are hindered by debilitating doubts that rob you of your faith, you can do the following exercises to develop your faith.

HOW TO DEVELOP FAITH

First, I suggest you bring order and understanding to your mind by creating an image to work with. Create this image in your conscious mind. (This is the part of you that thinks and reasons. Your free will lies here.) Use it to decide or make changes required to live the type of life you want. Be aware that your conscious mind can accept or reject any idea.

Impress this image of your choice on your subconscious mind. This is the spiritual side of your personality, and it knows no limits except those you consciously choose. This part of your personality will accept and carry out any order or thought your conscious mind has chosen to accept because it has no ability to reject it.

This part of your personality operates in an orderly manner, and it expresses itself in feelings and actions. Because of this, any thought you consciously choose to impress upon the subconscious through repetition becomes fixed in this part of your personality. This idea that is fixed will then continue to express itself without any conscious assistance from you.

Use affirmations in the form of repetitive orders to convince your subconscious mind to accept and believe that you will receive that for which you ask, and it will because it has no other option than to act on this belief. Because the subconscious mind has no ability to reject, it will pass back this belief to you in the form of faith.

It is also possible to accomplish this objective by playing a trick on yourself. You can tell yourself every day that you are already in possession of your goal by affirmations, repeatedly directing this instruction to your subconscious mind.

In this manner, you are continually impressing on the subconscious that this is the reality you're looking for, because faith can be induced or practiced by taking baby steps with repeated instructions to the subconscious mind through the principle of repetition or auto-suggestion.

Finally, the practice that develops faith starts with constant affirmation of orders to the subconscious mind, followed by action because as you continue to do this, you'll begin to see with your inner eye the real image of what you want to achieve. In other words, it can be compared to forcing yourself to see what you want, and this is what faith is all about.

Note that it may take some time for you to master this. But with persistence, you'll surely achieve the result and finally develop this powerful emotion of faith.

8. IT'S TIME TO LET GO AND LET GOD PLAY HIS ROLE.

These days, everyone has the desire to achieve one thing or another. Some people want to live in a certain way or be recognized by their peers for their own personal gratification based on their influence over other people. But in a real sense, everyone must have a purpose in life.

However, you must fully realize that no achievement, wealth, or position can endure unless it is built upon truth and justice. Any transaction that does not benefit all whom it affects cannot be sustained, succeed, or truly prosper, because God is truth and cares about justice.

I would therefore recommend that you carefully consider your goal, your ambition, and your desires to make sure that you eliminate envy, jealousy, hatred, resentment, selfishness, and negative attitudes toward others, because these can never bring you success.

Change them now by forgiving those who have offended you and seek forgiveness from those whom you have offended. Forgive yourself for past mistakes. But first and foremost, you must ask God to forgive all your shortcomings. This is the beginning of your journey to success.

Jesus commands us to love our neighbor as ourselves. Develop love for all humanity so as to please God such that He will mold your mind, body, and affairs according to His will for you. Choose and follow this path of love and all that you seek will be added unto you, for God is love and God is the supply.

Having set your affairs in order, you are now fully equipped for the divine plan of your life. Go ahead and log into the awesome spiritual reserve that lies within every human being. Connect to divine providence for all supply of every need.

Please do this through prayer or by your spoken word to trigger the movement that is going to take place between spirit and form, with and through you but originating from God.

For, it is written in the Scriptures in Proverbs 3:5–6: "Trust in the LORD with all your heart and lean not on your own understanding; In all your ways acknowledge Him, and He shall direct your paths."

Now that you have reoriented your mind to expect God's involvement in your affairs by His perfect work, *let go and let God* do the rest. You do not have to know the "when" or "how." Let Him surprise you with His unfolding plan for you.

Give thanks that you have already received in the invisible realm. Level up to a season of blessings by making active preparations through spoken gratitude for all you will receive in the visible realm.

Do not waver on your faith and belief, because God is just, and He will always work to bring about your ultimate good, even if it's hard sometimes. Be wise to guard this faith zealously as you would guard your most precious possession.

Finally, you can ask God for poise and strength to ensure that your faith is not eroded and imperiled by fear, pessimism, weak, downhearted, and negative thoughts. Rather, be uplifted because from now on, the battle is God's and not yours. Your duty is to stand still and witness the salvation of the Lord.

CHAPTER THREE

WHY DID GOD CREATE HUMANS?

The heavens and the earth portray the awesome glory of God.
Yet, of all that He created; it is mankind that God loves the most.

H ave you ever wondered why God created humans or why He created anything at all? According to the Scriptures, God is Lord of the heavens and the earth. He is not served and worshipped with the hands of men as though He needed anything, and neither does He need the rest of creation for anything.

Many people believe that God created humanity so that they would love Him, while some think that God created humans to serve Him. Others say God created humans to obey and glorify Him. Or maybe, after creating the earth and the plant and animal life, God felt lonely, so He created humans as the last to keep Him busy and occupied.

Because we are humans, it is a sweet and heartwarming sentiment to feel this way about God, but it's simply not true that He created people for any of those reasons. It is incorrect to believe that God needs humanity, because God is self-sustaining. He lacks nothing and needs nothing. Rather, it is humanity that needs God, for in Him we live, prosper, and have our being.

However, it is right and natural that we show our gratitude to God by loving Him and serving Him. It is even more important for humans to obey and glorify God because God did not need us—He chose us and even made us in His own image.

The Bible describes the making of humans as a well-thought-out, direct, and purposeful act of creation by God. Genesis 2:7 says, "And the LORD God formed man of the dust of the ground, and breathed into his nostrils the breath of life; and man became a living being."

If you pause for a moment to consider this information, you will realize that God, who Himself is a perfect being, created something in His own perfect image and likeness. And for this purpose, He created a being with intellect and will, combined with spiritual and physical capabilities.

God, who is the full embodiment of love and goodness, created humans with love—in fact with as much love as He has for Himself. This is even evident in humans who have experienced love, in that one can see they know love is not something to keep for themselves. People who know and feel love want to spread it around as much as they can, for they understand that love is not something that should ever be withheld. Even the exclusive love shared by a husband and wife is spread through having children.

But in the case of God, we are talking about infinite love. God created humans with love and with the intention of spreading this love based on goodness. In the Scriptures, it is also written that He created a paradise—earth—before creating humans and proceeded to place humans inside this paradise.

Further, the Bible says that the Creator of the heavens, the true God, the One who formed the earth, did not create it simply for nothing but formed it to be inhabited in a manner that illustrates His divine attributes. So, God's will to create and sustain the universe is without any doubt for the benefit of humanity. That is why He lovingly prepared the earth to be a beautiful and permanent home for the human family.

The Scriptures further explain that God made the earth not just for the first humans, Adam and Eve, but for their offspring as well. They were to work together as a family to take care of and expand the paradise until it covered the entire globe, and they were to carry out this work under the loving direction of their Heavenly Father.

To show His trust in the capabilities of humans, God said He would let them "have dominion over the fish of the sea, over the birds of the air, and over every living thing that moves on the earth."[5]

Finally, God blessed humans and instructed them to be fruitful and become many to fill the earth and subdue it. After that, the Bible says, "God saw everything that He had made, and indeed it was very good."[6]

In his letter to the early Christian congregation in First John 3:1, the Apostle John said, "Behold what manner of love the Father has bestowed on us, that we should be called children of God!" And that is what we are. Here John affirms that God created humans to enjoy life forever on earth and to know God as their loving Father.

---

[5]   Genesis 1:28.

[6]   Genesis 1:31.

Therefore, should you be asking why God created humans? He created them because of who He is. He created us out of love, because God is love.

The Bible has shown that love is the underlying factor explaining why God designed and created the universe the way it is and prepared the earth specially as a living abode for humans.

God's love for His children is real and selfless, and He pours it out upon the object of His affection (us) in the form of the air we breathe, the nature we enjoy, and in all the aspects of all that He gives to us, without demanding anything in return. His only reward is in the joy of giving.

So, God is love in manifestation, and He is inviting every person on this planet to partake of this love because He knows that if you follow the path of love, all things are added unto you. For, love is the greatest gift of all.

In the Scriptures, it is written in First Corinthians 13:4–8:

> Love suffers long and is kind; love does not envy; love does not parade itself, is not puffed up; does not behave rudely, does not seek its own, is not provoked, thinks no evil; does not rejoice in iniquity, but rejoices in the truth; bears all things, believes all things, hopes all things, endures all things. Love never fails. But whether there are prophecies, they will fail; whether there are tongues, they will cease; whether there is knowledge, it will vanish away.

Here the Bible makes clear how important it is that we actively seek to practice love and use it to unleash the vast potentials embedded within every person, which we inherited from our Heavenly Father, who is the perfect embodiment of love.

To really emphasize how essential love is, First Corinthians 13:13 says, "And now abide faith, hope, love, these three; but the greatest of these is love." Having read this from the Bible, I would say that God created us out of love, and love is not just the way, love is the *only* way.

To summarize this chapter; I am going to explain the awesome power of love and how you can tap into it to unleash the creative potential that should come naturally to every person if they choose, because we are all children of God, blessed equally through our divine right. We are all equal before God, and He makes no distinction between old and young, male and female, rich and poor, or able and disabled.

GOD'S POWER OF LOVE

There is an awesome potential lying deep inside each and every one of us. We are blessed with the ability to co-create and bring forth our desires if we align with God's will. We can do this because everything we need is available in God's riches in glory. In fact, all we need is already here on earth even before we are born, and the rest comes to us as gifts, along with the life we are given.

However, it seems many people do not realize their latent ability just waiting to be released. Some who are aware do not believe they are capable of achieving what they seek, while others do not know how or where to begin in their quest.

The signs of the modern system of things show a pattern of distracting factors that rob people of their ability to think and focus on what they really want. These distracting factors also divert attention toward many unrewarding rabbit holes that offer little or no dividends.

Too many people are busy chasing make-believe and time-wasting vices of the modern-day era, like Facebook, Twitter, Instagram, TikTok, TV news and binge television, and celebrity worship, all of which do not favor personal development.

But inasmuch as these activities may lead people astray, they cannot confine you to any particular unfavorable condition if you rouse yourself from this "soul sleep" of semi-reality and if you do not despair but remember who you truly are—a child of God.

We should always rejoice in the fact that God created us out of the abundance of His love. This love is available twenty-four-seven, non-stop, three hundred and sixty-five days of the year. Before our present time and even back in Bible times, people achieved extraordinary things by going directly to this source that is powered by love.

In the Scriptures, you can read a most compelling story of how Solomon asked God to grant him an obedient heart to judge and rule over his people, because he understood the power of God's love for His children. In First Kings 3:9, we understand that Solomon believed that the same love God used to create the earth, a galaxy, and the human body could also be used to bring about the fulfilment of his goal.

Further on this matter, the Bible says that God answered Solomon in First Kings 3:12–13:

> Behold, I have done according to your words; see, I have given
> you a wise and understanding heart, so that there has not been
> anyone like you before you, nor shall any like you arise after you.
> And I have also given you what you have not asked: both riches
> and honor, so that there shall not be anyone like you among the
> kings all your days.

It is a well-documented fact that after this discussion with God, Solomon went on to become the richest and wisest king the world has ever known.

Truly, the best part of this story is that even though God told Solomon to ask, Solomon's request was only in regard to his people and his desire to do good by them. And this love of Solomon for his people triggered God's love in abundance—beyond what Solomon asked for—because love begets love and more love.

I would remind you once more to focus on love. The Bible has already proven that the greatest gift of all is love, and we've seen how powerful love is because every good thing flows and works from this source and because, through love, we are created and sustained by God.

In this modern time, we are living through another example of achieving great things is found in the unique histories of modern-day international superpowers. The United States of America and the United Kingdom have prospered greatly from asking God's blessing.

In the United States, American president's past and present have invoked God to bless the United States of America. They have done this because they fully understand that, as it is written in the Bible, if you ask, "it will be given to you." America's founders looked to God as "the Supreme Judge of the world." And "Supreme Benefactor." Therefore, they have asked, asked, and asked again over the centuries, and guess what! The U.S. is the richest country in the history of the world. They themselves bear testimony to this fact by their own words when they say that their country is the greatest on earth. However, their protection by God's blessing diminishes as that nation turns further and further away from God, the source of their blessing.

Some might be tempted to simplify, trivialize, or even derive some childish pleasure from making fun of this theory, but the simple truth is that anything is possible if you ask directly from the source of pure potentiality. When you ask for what is within God's will, you will receive all the power, intelligence, and organizing ability He chooses to bestow on you, as He bestowed wealth and wisdom on Solomon. These gifts help you to succeed. God may even choose to give you gifts when you don't ask Him, like in Solomon's case, when God chose to give something, Solomon did not even ask for!

Another nation that understands this theory of asking God for His favor is the United Kingdom. During every ceremony and important occasion, they never fail to ask God to save their king or their queen. In fact, they are really asking God to love their monarch because they know that the act of saving is derived from love.

The people of the United Kingdom believe that if God saves their queen or their king, their kingdom will remain united, and their leader will be a benevolent ruler. This will, in turn, usher in wealth and security, and their land will prosper. And prosper they do! You don't have to look far to see that the United Kingdom is one of the most prosperous regions of the world. Their monarchy is doing alright, the kingdom is still united, and their royal family is one of the longest-surviving monarchies in Europe. This is another example that gives testimony to the blessings received when we ask from God—in this case, a whole kingdom asking from God.

I would recommend that you do the same and ask God to bless, protect, and favor you, because He makes no distinction. Just as He does for these superpowers, He'll do for you.

Speak to God every morning when you wake up and every evening before retiring for the day. Remind Him of who you are and draw attention to yourself and thank Him for His blessings. Follow Solomon's example of honoring who God is by acknowledging His mercy, His goodness, and His kindness. Then, ask for help to achieve your goals and overcome your problems. Do this and you'll see tremendous changes in your life. Real-life miracles will happen for you.

If you choose to remind yourself constantly of the unique act of thanking God for being the source of love and all goodness and asking Him to help you, then you will see how both in Bible times and in our modern times, God's power of love is made available to all without exception. The moment you ask is the moment this care and love from God in the form of force or power that is not human in origin will trigger all sorts of unexpected things to occur in your life.

This providence from God unleashes a whole stream of events that would never otherwise occur, releasing in one's favor all manner of material and spiritual assistance that no man could imagine would come his way.

Bear in mind when asking God for His favor that no person and no circumstance on earth can prevent you from receiving God's power of love, and it is free. You can use it to achieve greatness but remember where your greatness comes from. And consider how you can bless others with the blessings you receive from God?

Make it a practice to leave every person you speak to, with an impression of feeling good about coming in contact with you, for that is what God's power of love should truly reflect in you. Those you encounter should sense the Spirit of God working in you. Whatever you put out there in the form of love or kindness can multiply and come back to recharge you and start the cycle all over again, because the power of love is unstoppable.

PART TWO:

KING OF KINGS

CHAPTER FOUR

THE FALL OF MAN

A ll over the world, many people are worried about epidemics, environmental issues, unemployment, social inequality, corruption, and poverty. Because of their worry, they keep pondering why the conditions of living and why the environment and natural system of things of this modern world are progressively deteriorating instead of improving. In fact, it is not surprising to hear that the majority of people on earth are not happy.

For instance, the World Bank estimated in 2017 that more than two billion people are living in poverty. This shows that despite enormous gains in well-being and economic circumstances of hundreds of millions of people, a huge number of individuals, communities, and even entire countries are still trapped in poverty.

Therefore, the question many are asking is, how is it possible that while several millions of people are enjoying an affluent lifestyle, billions of people are also languishing in poverty today? Surprisingly, this trend is not only visible in undemocratic countries but in democratic nations of the world as well.

You will find poverty on all five continents of the world. It exists in developed and semi-developed regions of the world and even in first- and third-world countries as well. This situation is now dire, concerning, and embarrassing to world leaders to the extent that every year, members of the World Economic Forum and their invited guests meet in Switzerland, scratching their heads trying to figure out why poverty remains rife all over the world and how to end it.

I am obliged to state that poverty is not a consequence of limited global resources or even a burgeoning world population. It is a result of political and economic injustice that has been piling up over the centuries of human existence. It did not start today or in our lifetime. Rather, it has been allowed to multiply, fester, and become the painful reality of many people in our present system of things.

However, before I delve further into the myriads of problems faced by people all over the world, I must reaffirm that the purpose of writing this book is not to blame anyone or society for the sorry situation of things around the world. Rather, my sincere hope is that through this book, you'll transform your life by discovering the real source of a life of fulfillment as originally planned by God, whose main purpose is that His children multiply happily in a happy world.

Lest we forget, I would like to reemphasize that God created humans with love and compassion. He took time to design and create the earth to be perfect for human habitation, before placing Adam and Eve inside it with the instruction to be fruitful, fill the earth, and subdue it.

The Bible states clearly that God went on to say, "See, I have given you every herb that yields seed which is on the face of all the earth, and every tree whose fruit yields seed; to you it shall be for food. Also, to every beast of the earth, to every bird of the air, and to everything that creeps on the earth, in which there is life, I have given every green herb."[7]

Further, Scripture describes how God created a special place—the Garden of Eden—and proceeded to settle the first humans in it, instructing them to cultivate and take care of it.

However, God also commanded the man: "Of every tree of the garden you may freely eat; but of the tree of the knowledge of good and evil you shall not eat, for in the day that you eat of it you shall surely die."[8]

Yet, Adam and Eve did exactly what God commanded them *not* to do. The Bible describes accurately how Eve allowed herself to be persuaded by the serpent to eat the fruit from this tree. And after eating the fruit, she took it home to her husband and convinced him to eat the forbidden fruit also, thereby opening the floodgates to all the problems that torment mankind up until this present day.

But this incident has remained a great puzzle to mankind. Why did this perfect man, created in the image of God with the whole earth at his disposal, choose with his God-given free will to disobey God? Through that single act of eating the fruit from the tree of the knowledge of good and evil, every human being forfeited their perfection, thereby inviting sin, suffering, and death to take away all the beautiful plans God intended for us.

Because God had warned Adam of what would happen if he were to eat from this tree, God did not let Adam off the hook. Rather,

---

[7]   Genesis 1:29–30.

[8]   Genesis 2:16–17.

He allowed Adam to live the life he had chosen for himself and his offspring. This disobedient option is now the reality that the offspring of Adam and Eve are facing today in the form of poverty, corruption, injustice, immorality, pestilence, and death.

The Bible shows how God rebuked Adam in Genesis 3:17–19. God said to Adam:

> Because you have heeded the voice of your wife, and have eaten
> from the tree of which I commanded you, saying, "You shall
> not eat of it":
> Cursed is the ground for your sake;
> In toil you shall eat of it
> All the days of your life.
> Both thorns and thistles it shall bring forth for you,
> And you shall eat the herb of the field.
> In the sweat of your face you shall eat bread
> Till you return to the ground,
> For out of it you were taken;
> For dust you are,
> And to dust you shall return.

From a human perspective, I would say that in comparison to the gravity of the offense committed, Adam got away here with a suspended sentence. Despite his disobedience and the consequences that followed, God understood that His punishment would have a far-reaching effect on future generations following Adam and Eve. And sure enough, it has.

But God was lenient, for even after pronouncing His verdict, He made provisions that would enable the offspring of Adam and

Eve to redeem the lost glory of their forebears by accepting a life-insurance policy to protect themselves and their children yet to be born. God gave them a chance to regain and retain perfection, which was His original plan—that humans would not die but live a joyful and fulfilling life on earth.

This life-insurance policy for the offspring of Adam is revealed and foretold in the Bible, along with instructions on how anyone can benefit from it. But if they elect not to partake of that life insurance, they have to take a shot at ruling themselves, which was the choice of their forebears.

Because Adam and Eve foolishly exchanged the perfect life and the perfect plan God had for them for a piece of fruit, that disobedience turned out to be a costly mistake that continues to corrode, corrupt, and chip away at the perfection in God's most beloved creation—aka humans.

From then onwards, man was on his own, because he knew good and evil, but he still retained his free will from God to plot his own course and decide his own fate. It was then up to him to use his intelligence to control the vast earth and all other creatures in his habitat and look after the environment as well. And after this period, the rest of the history of mankind has been characterized by suffering resulting from the fall of man.

On that note, I will consult the Bible regularly to trace the beginning of the problems facing humanity today. To proceed, I would state without any doubt that the Bible is the only book that shows the accurate beginning of mankind. And in the system of things then, this predicament could be compared to navigating uncharted territory, because it was not known how humans were going to use their intelligence to take care of themselves. However, this marked the beginning of the rule of man.

THE RULE OF MAN

Mankind has come a long way since they moved out of the beautiful paradise of the Garden of Eden. Adam and Eve had to learn or improvise how to survive on their own in order to make shelter, provide food and clothing for themselves, make tools to hunt and tools to work the earth, and raise a family as well.

Since then, their offspring have multiplied exceedingly to fill the earth, and they have made significant advancements in the fields of medicine, arts, entertainment, science, and technology. They have also made laws, rules, and policies to govern all aspects of human activities on earth. Some of these laws have transformed into customs and traditions showcasing different cultures and attitudes of people from many parts of the earth.

However, the creation of laws, traditions and policies have also resulted in the elevation of some humans above other humans, thereby introducing a minority ruling class to govern a vast majority in different areas of the world.

This does not mean that human societies have no need for rules, regulations, and laws to function. Rather, it points to the fact that most of these laws have favored the ruler to the disadvantage of the ruled, and in most cases the ruler has usurped what was designed in good faith to ensure the progress of humanity and turned it instead into a burden for the rest of the people under his rulership.

Since the inception and acceptance of this type of existence with no binding adherence to theocratic principles, watered down by a loose human interpretation of the will of God, the good, the bad, and the ugly sides of the human character have been exposed to reveal the monumental price paid for the loss of human perfection. This costly price is continually paid by a vast majority of people all over the world in the present system of things.

But before I continue on the unfavorable reality for many people in this current system of things, I must point out that the progressive shift of human society, accompanied by the subsequent corruption and injustice experienced by many, started right from the very beginning, when one human being proclaimed and elevated himself above other humans to the position of mighty hunter, mighty warrior, and mighty king to be adored by his compatriots, whom he saw as subjects.

This was the pattern of rulers and kings in Bible times. Some of them were warriors who fought and defended their people from other tribes and contributed to the progress that carries on to our present day. Nonetheless, the progress they made was often achieved by committing atrocities, and they made decisions that were full of flaws both in the eyes of God and in the eyes of men.

The follies of such men were correctly recorded in the Bible as a testimony of leadership malfeasance for future generations to learn from. Some of these leaders rose to be rulers and kings of vast populations of people in Bible times.

Because of their roles in what carries on to this day, I will refer to them as "Bible kings."

Among these individuals, the name that stood out then was NIMROD.

The Bible shows clearly that there were kings in places like Assyria and Babylon going back to the far reaches of time. The first king is not mentioned, but Nimrod is the most notable named king among them.

Nimrod is described as king in the land of Shinar, also known as Mesopotamia. He is portrayed in Genesis 10:8–12 (ESV) as "the first on earth to be a mighty man. He was a mighty hunter before the LORD." He made the start in becoming a mighty one in the earth. But he displayed himself to be a mighty hunter in opposition to God.

From Shinar, he went on to build the cities of Nineveh and Babylon, which later grew to be a megacity in ancient times. As recorded in the Bible, it is in this area that the people attempted to construct the Tower of Babel in opposition to God. They said among themselves, "Come, let us build ourselves a city, and a tower whose top is in the heavens."[9] If Nimrod founded the city of Babel, it is likely he would have been part of this plan based on the goal of trying to reach heaven-with the aim of living next to God.

However, God did not approve of this plan. To make them stop in their inordinate intention, He confused their language that they might not be able to communicate with one another, and He subsequently scattered them all over the surface of the earth.

---

[9] Genesis 11:4.

This narrative in the Bible shows that being strong and powerful does not always correspond to being right with God. Because of this, Nimrod is fleetingly remembered in the Bible as a defiant, mighty warrior and a tyrannical and unreasonable king.

THE PHARAOHS OF EGYPT

The pharaohs were some of the early kings mentioned in the Bible. In ancient Egypt, the pharaoh was both the political and religious leader of the people, with the self-proclaimed titles "Lord of Upper and Lower Egypt," and "High Priest of the Temple" in all of their kingdom. In the early dynasties, some of them used to have two or three titles--the Horus, the Sedge and sometimes, the Bee. In today's optics, they will be simply referred to as the Czar.

The pharaohs proclaimed that their rulership was in accordance with the will of the gods, and in later dynasties, the pharaoh king projected himself to be associated with the divine. Their main duty was to ensure the unification of Upper and Lower Egypt and to defend their kingdom against enemies.

The pharaoh had the sacred duty to defend the borders of their land, but also to attack neighboring nations to take their natural resources. In their role as high priests of the temple, they built great monuments and pyramids, paying homage to the numerous gods of their land who they believed gave them power to rule in this life and probably guide them in the next.

The pharaohs ruled mainly by the maintenance of *ma'at*, a word meaning "harmony," and "balance," which had been decreed by the gods and had to be observed in order for their people to live the best possible life. Because of this, the pharaohs were considered gods on earth and the intermediaries between the gods and the people.

Because the pharaoh had absolute power, it was up to the individual ruler to interpret the will of the gods correctly and then act on it. Accordingly, they employed warfare and brutality regularly to restore balance and harmony (*ma'at*) in their land. They attacked and plundered neighboring lands as well if it was thought to be in the interest of harmony, according to the interpretation of the ruling pharaoh. And this was their pattern of rulership up until the arrival of Joseph the Israelite to the land of Egypt.

We may not know who the first pharaoh was, as this was not described in the Bible, and we do not know which Egyptian pharaoh challenged Moses—and God, who sent Moses to liberate the Israelites. But in the book of Exodus, this pharaoh is described as the principal villain.

Unlike the pharaoh who knew Joseph, the pharaoh in the time of Moses was cruel and vindictive and viewed the Israelites with disfavor. He made the sons of Israel slave under tyranny and continued making their life bitter with hard labor and every form of slavery in the fields where they were working.

This pharaoh introduced chiefs of forced labor for the main purpose of oppressing the Israelites in their burden bearing. The Israelites were deprived of straw to make the sun-dried bricks used in building the temples, monuments, and supply cities of Pithom and Rameses. Yet, the Israelites were expected to meet the daily quota of finished bricks that they were forced to produce.

The pharaoh even commanded the Hebrew midwives to put to death any male child that they helped the Hebrew women to deliver on the stool of childbirth. However, this plan did not work because these midwives feared God and refused to carry out this order.

Finally, pharaoh commanded his henchmen to throw every newborn Hebrew son into the River Nile. This was the law of the land when Moses was born to a certain man of the house of Levi. Moses's mother was able to hide Moses for a while, and then she built an ark to float on the Nile and placed him in it.

Exodus 2:1–10 describes how pharaoh's daughter found the child in the ark of papyrus among the reeds by the bank of the river Nile. She adopted this child so that he grew up to become a son to her, and she proceeded to call his name Moses, as she said, "because I drew him out of the water."[10]

Further in the book of Exodus, the Bible describes how God used Moses to free the Israelites from the tyrannical rule of this king after several requests to allow them to leave Egypt. In the end, this obstinate pharaoh finally gave in, after much punishment from God, and allowed the Israelites to depart.

This epic Bible story is concluded in Exodus 14:19–28, narrating how the Egyptians, their war chariots, their cavalrymen, and all of pharaoh's military forces that chased after the Israelites into the sea drowned. Not so much as one of them survived, while the sons and daughters of Israel crossed safely on dry land.

However, this human rule by the pharaohs could not last, because after the reign of Ramesses III, the power of the pharaohs began to decline, and they suffered a humiliating defeat at the hands of the

---

[10] Exodus 2:10.

Persians. Their dynasty ended when Egypt became a Roman province, thereby sweeping the tyranny, the glory, and the might of the pharaohs into faded memory.

KING NEBUCHADNEZZAR

In the entire history of human rulership, King Nebuchadnezzar is one of the most notorious villains portrayed in the Bible. He was the king of Babylon who constructed the hanging gardens of Babylon for his wife. Under his rule, the Neo-Babylonian Empire became one of the most powerful kingdoms in the world, and the city of Babylon grew into a formidable city.

According to the Bible, Nebuchadnezzar conquered Jerusalem and destroyed the temple built by Solomon. He plundered the city, took ten thousand people captive out of Judah, and forcibly transferred them to Babylon.

King Nebuchadnezzar was one of the most powerful men on earth then, and people of different nations, cultures, and religions were drawn to his empire. He was known to surround himself with thinkers and magicians and he employed wise men in his service. True to his nature, when he took the Jews captive, he selected the young men with the most potential and tried to brain-wash them by having them schooled in the wisdom of Babylon.

Among the Jews he chose was the Prophet Daniel, as well as Hananiah, Mishael, and Azariah, who are better known by the names Nebuchadnezzar gave them. He changed their names to Belteshazzar, Shadrach, Meshach, and Abednego.

In the book of Daniel, the Bible narrates how King Nebuchadnezzar was plagued by a dream and wanted someone to interpret it for him. So, he summoned magicians, sorcerers, and astrologers and asked them to interpret his dream. But first, he insisted that they tell him what he had seen in his dream.

Nebuchadnezzar fancied himself smart, thinking that only someone who knew what the dream was without being told could accurately interpret it. But what he asked them to interpret went far beyond the discerning and magical powers of these charlatans.

After they told him that his dream was beyond human interpretation, he decided to execute all the wise men in Babylon, including the young Jewish men under his tutelage.

However, when Daniel learned they were all going to die because no one knew what the king's dream was or what it meant, he asked Nebuchadnezzar not to kill anyone yet and asked for time to discern this dream.

Daniel went back to his friends, Hananiah, Mishael, and Azariah, and asked them to pray for God to reveal the dream out of mercy. God listened to their prayer and revealed the dream and its interpretation to Daniel, and he explained it to Nebuchadnezzar. You can read this in Daniel 2:31–45. Daniel's ability to interpret the king's dream without being told what it was revealed a wisdom none of the king's wise men possessed. It showed Daniel's wisdom came from God, and as a result of this, King Nebuchadnezzar appointed Daniel ruler of the city of Babylon and awarded high positions to his friends, Shadrach, Meshach, and Abednego, as well.

But this was just the beginning of the complicated relationship between Daniel and Nebuchadnezzar, and this would not be the last time Daniel would interpret a dream for this pompous king. What none of them understood at that time, as the Bible narrative reveals, is that God was using Daniel and his friends to reveal His own glory and power, which far surpassed that of the powerful king of Babylon.

Shortly after this period, Nebuchadnezzar made a massive golden statue and commanded people of all nations to bow down and worship this idol or else be thrown into a furnace. Shadrach, Meshach, and Abednego refused to bow down to this statue, to the consternation of the king's other wise men.

King Nebuchadnezzar gave them another chance to worship the statue and asked them, "Who is the god who will deliver you out of my hands?"

They replied: "O Nebuchadnezzar, we have no need to answer you in this matter. If this be so, our God whom we serve is able to deliver us from the burning fiery furnace, and He will deliver us out of your hand, O king. But if not, be it known to you, O king, that we will not serve your gods or worship the golden image that you have set up."

Their answer infuriated Nebuchadnezzar, and he responded by cranking up the heat on the furnace, binding them up, and throwing them into the furnace. The furnace was so hot it killed the men who threw them in.

In this part of the story, the Bible describes a spectacular occurrence in which the king famously remarked: "I see four men unbound, walking in the midst of the fire, and they are not hurt; and the appearance of the fourth is like a son of the gods."

Subsequently, Nebuchadnezzar told Shadrach, Meshach, and Abednego to come out of the furnace. They were miraculously unscathed. The king therefore commanded that anyone who said anything against their God would be dismembered.[11]

But King Nebuchadnezzar did not learn anything from this lesson, and he continued carrying on in his bombastic ways. God was not finished with him, for he had to be taught a bitter lesson in humility.

In Daniel 4:4–37 (ESV), the Bible describes how King Nebuchadnezzar descended into madness. It all started when he had another dream, which he asked Daniel to interpret as he had done before. Only this time, he told Daniel what he had dreamed.

In his dream this time around, he saw a tree so enormous that "its top reached to heaven." Its leaves were beautiful, its fruit was abundant, and it sheltered and fed every creature. And then an angel came along and commanded that the tree be cut down, all the branches chopped off, and its foliage shaken off.

The angel said, "Let the beasts flee from under it and the birds from its branches." Furthermore, the angel commanded that the stump and roots of this tree be bound with iron and bronze and remain in the ground, in the grass of the field.

> Let him be wet with the dew of heaven. Let his portion be with the beasts in the grass of the earth. Let his mind be changed from a man's, and let a beast's mind be given to him; and let seven periods of time pass over him.

---

[11]   Daniel 3 ESV.

Finally, the angel said, "The sentence is by the decree of the watchers, the decision by the word of the holy ones, to the end that the living may know that the Most High rules the kingdom of men and gives it to whom He will and sets over it the lowliest of men."

After listening to this frightful dream, Daniel told Nebuchadnezzar that he, Nebuchadnezzar, was the tree, and he would go insane until he acknowledged the God of Israel. Therefore, Daniel gave him this advice: "Break off your sins by practicing righteousness, and your iniquities by showing mercy to the oppressed, that there may perhaps be a lengthening of your prosperity."

And just as Daniel had told the king, one year later, Nebuchadnezzar lost his mind like the dream said.

In Daniel 4:33, the Scriptures say regarding the condition of Nebuchadnezzar that:

> He was driven from among men and ate grass like an ox, and his body was wet with the dew of heaven till his hair grew as long as eagles' feathers, and his nails were like birds' claws.

As if on cue, it so happened that after a period of "seven times," or seven months, Nebuchadnezzar's sanity was restored at the moment he acknowledged the sovereignty of God by his own mouth, proclaiming:

> His dominion is an everlasting dominion,
> and His kingdom endures from generation to generation;
> all the inhabitants of the earth are accounted as nothing,
> and He does according to His will among the host of heaven
> and among the inhabitants of the earth;

and none can stay His hand
or say to Him, "What have You done?"

After this proclamation, God forgave Nebuchadnezzar, and he was restored to his throne. He became even greater than he had been before this lesson.

And finally, Nebuchadnezzar gave a testimony to the awesome power of God, saying:

> Now I, Nebuchadnezzar, praise and extol and honor the King of heaven, for all His works are right and His ways are just; and those who walk in pride He is able to humble.

This compelling story about Nebuchadnezzar should serve as a constant reminder to all that if God can forgive this pompous king, then God will forgive everyone who renounces his or her sins by doing what is right.

CHAPTER FIVE

KINGS OF ISRAEL

SAUL

Saul was the son of Kish from the tribe of Benjamin. He came from a wealthy family, and he was tall, dark, and handsome in appearance. In fact, the Scriptures state that "there was not a more handsome person than he among the children of Israel. From his shoulders upward he was taller than any of the people."[12] Saul was chosen to be the first king of Israel.

However, Saul was an ordinary man before he was anointed as king over Israel. Before this time, the nation of Israel had been a scattered collection of tribes that did not have a central leader and no formal government other than God, who had rescued them from the despotic rule of the pharaoh of Egypt. God had provided Israel with prophets who served as religious leaders but not as kings.

After the Israelites left Egypt, they lived in turbulent times and were under the constant threat of war. The Philistines were Israel's sworn enemy, and war broke out between the two on a fairly regular

---

[12]   First Samuel 9:2.

basis. Because of the constant threat of war, the people wanted to become like the nations surrounding them.

But the rulership of one person over the vast majority was not the way of the Israelites. This is because, many years before Saul's rule and during the time of the judges, Israel was loosely governed by judges who presided over domestic disputes and were not equipped to rule in times of war. In times of trouble, a leader would arise, but none of these leaders ever consolidated the power of the twelve tribes of Israel into one nation.

During this period, Samuel the prophet was Israel's religious leader. When he got old, he appointed his sons as judges over Israel. But his sons did not walk in his ways, as they turned out to be good-for-nothing men.

Because of this, the people pressed Samuel to appoint a king to rule over them. This request was displeasing to Samuel, and because he was deeply suspicious of monarchy, he interpreted the people's demand as a rejection of the idea of God being their leader.

Samuel consulted God, and although God directed him to "heed the voice of the people in all that they say to you,"[13] Samuel felt obliged to warn them and show them the ways of a king.

The Prophet Samuel predicted that a king:

- Would impose heavy taxes on the people.
- Would demand forced labor of the common people, thus making slaves of them.

---

[13]   First Samuel 8:7.

- Would establish a standing army by compelling men to carry arms and be professional soldiers.
- Would expropriate property to enrich himself and to give to his cohorts and servants.

Samuel's warning became a famous prediction about monarchy and human leaders that turned out to be true, and this trend persists up until our present day.

But Samuel was a servant of God. Thus, it became his task to anoint a king from among the people. Samuel was also a wise and discreet man, so at first, he anointed Saul as king privately and without fanfare, and later it was made public.

In First Samuel 10:1, the Scriptures say: "Then Samuel took a flask of oil and poured it on his head and kissed him and said, 'Has not the LORD anointed you to be prince over His people Israel?'" Further, Samuel blessed him and said, "You shall reign over the people of the LORD and you will save them from the hand of their surrounding enemies. And this shall be the sign to you that the LORD has anointed you to be prince over His heritage" (ESV).

At this point, the Scriptures describe Saul as being so humble that he did not tell his relatives about his anointing as king over the nation of Israel. But Samuel gathered the people together and cast lots before them to confirm who was king and later announced that Saul had won.

Saul's reign over Israel started peacefully. However, within a short period, war had broken out between the Israelites and the Ammonites, and he joined his forces with the men of Jabesh at the battle of Gilead, where he inflicted a crushing defeat on the Ammonites.

From then on, Saul led the nation of Israel through several more military victories, and his popularity reached its zenith. However, he made a series of very serious blunders, beginning with an unauthorized sacrificial offering. After winning an important military victory, Saul did not pray but instead gave in to pride, disobeyed the Lord, and took Samuel's place at the altar. His downward spiral continued as he failed to eliminate all of the Amalekites and their livestock as commanded by God.

Moreover, he disregarded a direct order from God by deciding to spare the life of King Agag, along with some choice livestock. Further, he tried to cover up his transgression by lying to Samuel and, in essence, lying to God.

This disobedience proved to be the last straw, because soon after, God withdrew His Spirit from Saul, and Saul's life spiraled out of control. Even though he managed to continue as king, he was plagued by an evil spirit that tormented him and brought about waves of madness as he endured periods of deep manic depression.

He later took his own life after learning of the death of his sons at the hands of the Philistines.

Saul had it all. Good looks, height, charm, and leadership ability. He was chosen by God and given the opportunity to be Israel's first king. But his insistent disobedience against God led to his downfall.

In the Scriptures, the book of First Samuel describes accurately the rise and fall of King Saul and the lessons we can learn from his life. The most important is to obey the Lord, seek to do His will, and not to misuse the power given to us.

The irreparable break between God and Saul is arguably one of the saddest occurrences in the Bible.

KING DAVID

David was the youngest son of Jesse, from the city of Bethlehem. He was a young shepherd boy when Samuel sought him out and anointed him with oil in the midst of his father and brothers, signifying that God had chosen him to rule as king over Israel.

According to the Scriptures, because of King Saul's disobedience, God rejected Saul as king and decided to choose someone else. So, God sent Samuel to Jesse of Bethlehem, telling Samuel to fill his horn with oil because God had chosen among the sons of Jesse a king for Himself.

When Samuel arrived in Bethlehem at the house of Jesse, he saw Eliab, David's oldest brother. He thought surely this was the chosen one. But God told Samuel, "Do not look at his appearance or at his physical stature, because I have refused him. For the LORD does not see as man sees; for man looks at the outward appearance, but the LORD looks at the heart."[14]

Seven of Jesse's sons passed before Samuel, but God chose none of them. So, Samuel asked Jesse if he had any more sons. It happened that at that time, the youngest son, David, was out in the fields, tending sheep. Accordingly, he was called in from the fields.

When David appeared, he looked ruddy, with beautiful eyes and handsome appearance. God told Samuel, "Arise, anoint him; for this

---

[14]   First Samuel 16:7.

is the one."[15] Samuel took the horn of oil and anointed him, and from that day onward, the Spirit of the Lord came powerfully upon David.

Saul was still the king of Israel when David was anointed by Samuel, but the Spirit of the Lord had departed from Saul, and he was constantly tormented by an evil spirit. Because of this, Saul's servants suggested a harpist, and one of them recommended David, saying, "I have seen a son of Jesse the Bethlehemite, who is skillful in playing, a mighty man of valor, a man of war, prudent in speech, and a handsome person; and the LORD is with him."[16]

Thus, David was invited by Saul's servant, and he came into the king's service. David became a soothing influence on the troubled king by playing music that temporarily restored the king's sanity. Because of this, Saul was pleased with David, and David became one of his armor bearers.

However, Saul's pleasure in David vanished quickly as David rose in strength and fame by becoming a fine military leader.

In one of the best-known dramatic Biblical accounts, the Philistines were at war with the Israelites, and they taunted Israel's military forces with their champion—the giant Goliath. The Philistines proposed a duel between Goliath and any Israelite who would dare to fight him. But no one in Israel volunteered to fight the giant.

Goliath had been taunting the Israelites for forty days. It happened that David's older brothers were part of Saul's army, and David was visiting them at the battlefield when he heard the Philistine's boasts. So, David asked, "What shall be done for the man who kills this Philistine

---

[15]   First Samuel 16:12.
[16]   First Samuel 16:18.

and takes away the reproach from Israel? For who is this uncircumcised Philistine, that he should defy the armies of the living God?"[17]

King Saul heard what David was saying and sent for him. When David appeared before Saul, he said, "Let no man's heart fail because of him; your servant will go and fight with this Philistine."[18] But Saul was worried for David because he was not a trained soldier, and Goliath had been a warrior from his youth.

David assured Saul that he would prevail against the Philistine, just like he killed both a lion and a bear that had attacked his sheep in the fields. Further, David promised that Goliath would become like one of those beasts because he had defied the army of the living God, saying: "The LORD, who delivered me from the paw of the lion and from the paw of the bear, He will deliver me from the hand of this Philistine."[19]

Saul agreed on the condition that David wore his armor into the fight. But David was not used to the weight of the armor, so he left it behind. David took with him only his staff, his shepherd's bag, five smooth stones, and a sling.

Goliath was not intimidated by David, but neither was David intimidated by Goliath. David said to the Philistine giant, "You come to me with a sword, with a spear, and with a javelin. But I come to you in the name of the LORD of hosts, the God of the armies of Israel, whom you have defied. This day the LORD will deliver you into my hand, and I will strike you and take your head from you."[20]

---

[17] First Samuel 17:26.

[18] First Samuel 17:32.

[19] First Samuel 17:37.

[20] First Samuel 17:45–46.

So, it happened that when Goliath arose and drew near to meet David, David also ran to meet the giant. Then David put his hand in his bag and took out a stone. He placed the stone in the sling and slung it hard, and it struck Goliath in his forehead so that the stone bore into his forehead and he fell on his face to the ground.

But there was no sword in the hand of David. Therefore, David ran and stood over Goliath, took hold of his sword, drew it out of its sheath, killed Goliath, and cut off his head with it. When the Philistines saw that their champion was dead, they scattered and fled.

After killing Goliath, David entered into Saul's service full time. But then, Saul realized that God was with David, as he continued to grow in fame, causing people to sing praises of David. As a result of this, Saul became enraged and was consumed by a raging jealousy that drove him relentlessly to try to kill David at every opportunity. Because of this jealous hangover, David spent many years of his life fleeing from Saul.

Although King Saul never stopped pursuing him, David never raised his hand against his king and God's anointed, even when he had the opportunity to kill Saul. While on the run, David raised a mighty army. With God on his side, he defeated everyone in his path, always asking God first for permission and blessing before going into battle.

When Saul eventually died, David mourned him and his sons who had died in battle with him. After Saul's death, David was publicly anointed king over the house of Judah, and he then fought against the remaining sons of Saul, whom he defeated before being anointed king over all of Israel.

In the Bible, the second book of Samuel and first book of Kings describe in detail the exploits of David and all he was able to accomplish because God was with him. When King David wanted to build a temple for the Lord, the Prophet Nathan first told David to do as he wanted. But then God told Nathan that David would not be the one to build His temple.

Instead, God promised to build a house for David. This promise included the prediction that David's son Solomon would be the one to build the temple and hinted for the first time of a future Messiah, a son of David who would reign forever. And because of this, David made preparations for the temple before he died.

God's reason for not allowing David to build the temple was that he had shed so much blood, while David's son was to be a man of peace and not a man of war.

The Scriptures give an accurate account showing that much of David's shedding of blood was a result of war. But in a sordid incident of human weakness, David had one of his commanders killed. It occurred that while his men were at war on one occasion, David remained home. From his rooftop, he saw a beautiful woman bathing. When he inquired, he found out that she was Bathsheba, the wife of Uriah the Hittite, one of his commanders who was at war. Still, David sent his messengers for her. When she came to David, he slept with her, and she became pregnant.

Because he made her pregnant, David called Uriah back from battle, hoping he would sleep with his wife and believe the child to be his. But Uriah refused to go home while his comrades were still on the battlefield.

So, David arranged for Uriah to be killed in battle, thereby paving the way for him to marry his commander's wife, Bathsheba.

When the Prophet Nathan confronted David about his sin with Bathsheba, David responded in shame and repentance and showed character through humility and remorse, because his true heart was for God. However, Nathan told David that his son with Bathsheba would die as a result of this sin. And when God enforced His judgment, David accepted it completely despite his sorrow over the loss of his son.

This unflattering story of David's slip up and his exercise of poor judgement teaches us that even though he was a man after God's own heart, he was also human and sinful. This incident in his life shows us that no human is perfect, and even those we hold in high esteem struggle with sin. It also serves as a warning about temptation and the way sin can quickly multiply and lead to serious suffering.

In this story, we also see God's love and kindness, because Solomon, David's son who succeeded him, was also born to Bathsheba, and it was through Solomon's line that Jesus descended.

Finally, David will be fondly remembered by many generations as the great king of Israel who wrote many of the psalms in the Bible. And in his poems, we can see that he sought after God and glorified Him.

KING SOLOMON

Solomon was born as the son of King David, and he succeeded his father to the throne of Israel. He was born to David and Bathsheba after the death of their son conceived through adultery.

When he was a boy, his father, King David, entrusted Solomon to the Prophet Nathan to train him in the ways of God. Nathan called him by the name Jedidiah, which means "beloved of God."

God gifted Solomon with unsurpassed wisdom, and because of this, he was known as the wisest man who ever lived. He was also famously known as the king who built the first temple of Jerusalem, as well as being the richest man who ever lived.

In the Scriptures, it is noted that Solomon was not the firstborn son of his father, and therefore, he was not in line to become the heir to King David's throne. However, because of God's instruction that Solomon would sit on the throne after him, David was determined that Solomon would succeed him instead of his elder sons. Solomon was anointed as king while David, his father, was still alive, and this infuriated his half-brother Adonijah, who tried forcibly to take the throne from him but was unsuccessful.

Not long after Solomon was anointed as king, God visited him in a dream and told Solomon to ask for what He should give him. Solomon replied, saying, "Now, O LORD my God, You have made your servant king instead of my father David, but I am a little child; I do not know how to go out or come in. And Your servant is in the midst of Your people whom You have chosen, a great people, too numerous to be numbered or counted. Therefore, give to Your servant an understanding heart to judge Your people, that I may discern between good and evil. For who is able to judge this great people of Yours?"[21]

---

[21]   First Kings 3:7–9.

God was pleased that Solomon had asked for this. So, God said to him, "Because you have asked this thing, and have not asked long life for yourself, nor have asked riches for yourself, nor have asked the life of your enemies, but have asked for yourself understanding to discern justice, behold, I have done according to your words."[22]

Further, God said that He would give Solomon a wise and understanding heart so that there would never be anyone like him. God added that He would also give Solomon what he did *not* ask for—great riches and honor such that in his lifetime, he would have no equal among kings.

God concluded by saying that if Solomon walked in obedience and kept His laws and commands as David his father did, that God would give him a long life. Then Solomon awoke and realized it had been a dream. However, Solomon went to Jerusalem and stood before the ark of the covenant of the Lord and made offerings and a feast for all his servants.

Shortly after this incident, the wisdom that God had given Solomon was demonstrated. It happened while judging a case between two women who each claimed they were the mother of the same newborn baby.

The Bible, in First Kings 3:16–28, describes a situation where both women had newborn babies and one of the babies died in the night. So, the mother of the dead baby swapped the babies. And when the women woke up in the morning, they started fighting over the baby that was alive. Each woman claimed that the living baby was hers.

---

[22]   First Kings 3:11–12.

When they were brought to King Solomon, the two women kept arguing. Then Solomon said, "The one says, 'This is my son, who lives, and your son is the dead one'; and the other says, 'No! But your son is the dead one, and my son is the living one.'"

So, Solomon said, "Bring me a sword," and they brought a sword for the king. He then gave the order to cut the living child in two and give half to one and half to the other. However, the real mother of the living child was deeply moved out of love for her son and said to the king, "O my lord, give her the living child, and by no means kill him!"

But the other woman said, "Let him be neither mine nor yours, but divide him." Then Solomon gave his ruling: "Give the first woman the living child, and by no means kill him; she is his mother."

King Solomon declared that the woman who cried out was the real mother because she would rather give up her baby so that he would live than see him killed. And because of this judgement, many people were astounded by Solomon's wisdom.

Solomon was king of Israel for forty years, and during this time there was peace and unity, and the people prospered like never before. He masterminded massive building projects and built the great temple of Jerusalem, about which his father, David, had left instructions regarding how God wanted it built.

Solomon signed treaties and agreements with neighboring kings and developed successful commerce that made him the wealthiest king of his time. He possessed a fleet of ships that would come in every three years carrying gold, silver, and ivory, and he came to have 1,400 chariots and 12,000 steeds. And all of this was made possible through his partnership with neighboring kings, tribute money paid to him, and heavy taxation.

In the Scriptures, First Kings 10:23–25 describes King Solomon as a king greater in riches and wisdom than all the other kings of the earth. All the people of the earth were seeking Solomon to hear the wisdom that God had put in his heart.

These visitors brought with them gifts of articles of silver and gold and mules and horses, while others brought with them spices, ornaments, and special metals. And everyone who came to visit inquired of King Solomon's wisdom.

However, Solomon was also a womanizer. In order to make peace with the pharaoh, he married his daughter and built a palace for her. He could not control his lust, as he went on to marry seven hundred women, as well as having three hundred concubines, or mistresses.

Many of Solomon's women worshiped idols and false gods, and this had a negative impact on his life. Inevitably, Solomon was lured away from God into the worship of false gods. He developed an inordinate desire for adulterous relationships that eventually caused the loss of many blessings from God.

Because of his polygamy and lavish lifestyle, his time became more consumed with worldly and idolatrous entertainment. This attitude caused Solomon to ignore the Lord's directive, and this angered God. Therefore, the Lord raised up armies to attack and take away a large part of his kingdom.

But God did not forsake Solomon. He allowed this to happen to remind Solomon to keep walking in God's ways, because his wayward actions had greatly influenced the kingdom in a negative way, to the extent that idolatry was openly practiced in Israel.

Despite these follies, Solomon loved God, and he is fondly remembered for writing a great amount of the Scriptures. He wrote Ecclesiastes, Song of Solomon, Proverbs, and parts of the books of Kings. And his skills in diplomacy, architecture, and management brought peace to his kingdom and transformed Jerusalem into one of the most important cities of that era.

Today in our present system of things, there are lessons we can learn from Solomon:

- First, when we seek to do God's will, He will provide a way for it to be accomplished by giving us the wisdom and providing the help, opportunity, and protection to carry it to successful completion.
- When God is for us, nothing can prevail against us.
- Despite God's provision for our salvation, wants, and needs, we can make bad choices because we still have imperfection inherited from Adam. This imperfection in the form of fleshly desires will constantly want to rebel against what God tells us to do.

Therefore, it is wise to remember the mistakes of Solomon because they speak loudly to us in our current-day materialistic culture. When we worship possessions, the satisfaction of the flesh, and fame over God, we are headed for a fall.

CHAPTER SIX

MEDIEVAL KINGS

Truly, this only I have found: that God made man upright,
but they have sought out many schemes. (Ecclesiastes 7:29)

From the very beginning when Adam and Eve left the Garden of Eden to fend for themselves, mankind has been running away from the reality that we humans cannot rule ourselves as well as God can rule us if we remain obedient. This is the truth we must accept when we consider that in both the past and the present, most kings and other human leaders have turned out to be selfish, vain, fickle minded, and unreliable.

Rather than face this truth, humans have chosen to trust the make-believe that we can rule ourselves. And because of this attitude, we have grown overconfident in our human ability, and this has resulted in the introduction of difficult solutions to solve simple problems.

For instance, humans still do not understand when enough is enough, and we still believe that lofty achievements based on pride, power, and might are more valuable than our human relationships or even our relationship with God.

Because of this narrow-minded way of reasoning, we have continued to create more problems and continued to prolong and compound the multitude of issues facing mankind from those early days up until the twenty-first-century world of today. However, nothing lasts forever, and this way of life that has proven unsustainable is surely and gradually coming to an end.

But before the time arrives to say "game over" for this system of things, it would be wise to trace this downward spiral of human leaders misruling other human beings to their disadvantage by going back in time before our modern era. Has there been any king or ruler who has ruled according to God's plan for people and God's plan for the earth as well?

In the previous chapter, we saw that even in Bible times—in those early days of human rulership—human leaders made serious mistakes and committed acts that were detrimental to the people they ruled and also to themselves.

But this pattern of governance did not stop there. The remnants of that system were carried over into the medieval period of human history in almost every part of the world. And even though there were some modifications, these modifications were more of a sinister kind for the ruled, benefiting the ruler and his henchmen.

In medieval times, there were kings and sometimes queens who ruled over a land, territory, or country. In Europe, Asia, Africa, and North and South America, the role of a king was to own land, lead his people in times of peace and war, and set laws. But often, this was not what occurred. Many of them lived a lavish lifestyle like virtual gods and enjoyed unimaginable, limitless wealth and power in their kingdoms. So, in terms of power, wealth, and privilege, there was no other social tier that rivalled the position of a king. In fact, it was good to be king in medieval times.

However, when we consider the ways and methods of kings in the system of things of that era, you will also see a continuous pattern of misrule, needless wars, and pervasive immorality. Because this condition controlled their way of life, people lived in fear, abject poverty, sickness, and hopelessness. Many had no way out due to widespread illiteracy and ignorance that kept them chained to their lowly positions.

This situation was very much to the advantage of the king and his cohorts, especially in the late Middle Ages and the period thereafter. Here is an example:

EUROPE

The tradition of the times gave the king great authority because it was said that God granted the king the seat of power. Due to this line of reasoning, the king aligned himself with the Church hierarchy, knowing fully that obedience to religious authority was pervasive amongst the people, and hence, if God chose the king, the people would obey without question.

Many of the kings, then, misused and abused their positions because whatever they did or however, they behaved instantly became the law and the accepted way of the land. In fact, the king had the right to go into any house in his kingdom, take anything that was in that house, enjoy the favors of any female in that house, and stay at the owner's expense for as long as he wished.

Similar to Bible times and our modern times, medieval kings lived in large castles and owned large estates. They maintained magnificent and luxurious wardrobes, and they enjoyed fine foods and drank choice wines while the majority of the people wallowed in extreme poverty.

In medieval times, the rulers had absolute power and authority over the people they ruled and enlisted the help of other people within their kingdoms. Notably, medieval kings of Europe allowed lords, barons, knights, and other favored members of society to live on their lands on the condition that they helped to form and mobilize armies for the kings when necessary and to collect taxes from the farming, fishing, and other economic activities of their subjects.

Due to constant disputes and wars, the king would lead these barons, knights, and lords along with their men into battles against neighboring kingdoms, and in most cases when disputes arose, the king was the sole individual responsible for dishing out justice as he saw fit.

But this is not a complete picture of what the life of a king in medieval times was all about. Like those in power today, the job of a king was a busy one. Even in periods of relative stability, there were constant threats to the kingdom both from within and outside the kingdom, and they had to deal with economic issues as well as the many internal political intrigues and struggles that life at the court of the king encourages.

Sometimes the alliance with the Church became untenable and turned into a pressure point for the king because the Church was a powerful political force, and the struggle for power between the king and the Church authorities made it difficult for a healthy and unified religious devotion.

However, there were a few exceptional kings of medieval times that concerned themselves with loftier goals than the gratification of their base desires. Some of them devoted themselves to grandiose, religious quests, such as the Crusades, while others built magnificent churches and places of worship.

Among the medieval kings were also men who were passionate about learning and men who promoted arts, culture, and other noble aspects of society, which they helped to nurture and develop during their time in power. A good example of this can be found in the very fact that the most well-known translation of the Bible is called the "King James version." This edition of the Bible was sponsored by King James of England, who helped and encouraged many to study things such as science, literature, and art. His contribution made the Bible affordable and available for common people.

This shows that some kings of medieval times had good agendas and accomplished important things for their kingdoms and for society in general. We should be grateful today because the good work these kings did helped to raise the standard of education and the standard of living for many people.

On the other hand, as we appreciate the noble efforts of a few medieval kings, it is noteworthy that the system of things in this period was mostly characterized and dominated by numerous kingdoms, each striving to outdo the other to become the wealthiest and the most powerful.

In order to achieve this status, the monarchs began to consolidate the smaller regional kingdoms in an attempt to create vast empires. This resulted in various wars and alliances among kings and nobles within the same region and further abroad. Because of this pervasive twisted way of thinking, greed, avarice, and nepotism became the cornerstones used to lay the foundation of medieval politics—a highly variable and unstable form of political structure that can be found in some countries even in our present time.

This political structure had no room for the most important duty of any ruler, which is to be his brother's keeper and to serve the people he is called to lead. And, similar to modern-day rulers, medieval kings had considerable amounts of power and authority that they used to carry out their personal agendas. They favored only those who were useful to them and corrupted some who might oppose them. This resulted in a feudal society where men who were appointed nobles by kings ruled over common people, working their land with impunity and levying heavy taxes on landless peasants.

Sometimes, a noble would require all male peasants over the age of eighteen to report for military service in the name of the king. It didn't matter if it was a justified war against a serious external threat or just a petty fight against a local rival. If you were called up for duty, you had to report for service, or you'd be hounded as a traitor.

During this period in Europe, kings also appointed barons, whom they corrupted by leasing lands to them and forcing them to swear an oath of allegiance to the king. These men who leased land from the king became wealthy and powerful and exerted complete control over the people and land they leased from the king, thereby creating enormous gaps between the rulers and the ruled.

These barons became executors of the feudal system, and they established their own systems of justice and tax collection. In return for the land and privilege they had been given, they paid rents and provided the king with men to serve as fighters and general security.

In this period, many barons were very rich and lived in opulent houses known as manors. Because of this, many of them were referred to as the "lord of the manor." They had their fingers in every pie baked by the common people, and many of them willingly engaged in nefarious activities in order to accumulate wealth. In fact, many of the organized-crime syndicates of our time copied their modus operandi from the barons of old.

However, the medieval period—the Middle Ages and the period known as the Renaissance that followed—would not be complete without mentioning the role of religion and the role of the Church in perpetuating the most unequal and unfavorable relationships between the rulers and the ruled.

This situation was inevitable because, in order to hold on to power, many kings of this period signed treaties and agreements with the churches in Europe and accepted many religious dogmas, introducing these as laws or as punishments against purported offenders—thereby placing extra burdens on the people.

An infamous example of this was the introduction of the law against *hexerei*, or witchcraft. This law ushered in one of the darkest episodes in human history—the witch-hunt hysteria and inquisition that ravaged Europe many centuries ago. After the introduction of this law, several thousands of people were executed by burning across Europe. Notable among these individuals were Jacques de Molay, Jan Hus, Joan of Arc, Patrick Hamilton, and William Tyndale.

The English monarch Mary I was known to have ordered hundreds of Protestants to be burned at the stake during her reign, in what would later be referred to as the "Marian Persecutions." Because of this, she was known as "Bloody Mary." Regrettably, many of these people were executed on trumped-up charges. As kings and their cohorts became more and more compromised in their relationship with the Church, this calamity was accepted and endorsed by the state and the Church. This resulted in the persecution of many accused individuals and the burning alive of humans openly in public places because of their beliefs or outspokenness against the authorities.

Sadly, these burnings were sanctioned by the Church hierarchy, and oftentimes, the most educated members of the society--who are supposed to know better, stridently demanded no mercy for the accused persons because their perceived crimes were allegedly feats of the devil.

The combined acts of persecution by the state and Church were the hammers used in breaking the will of the people in this period, and sanctioned injustice was meted out on individuals who dared to question or think differently regarding the deplorable condition of the common people.

Once the state and Church had become as thick as thieves, all the ugly aspects of human rulership began to crawl out from the dark, wicked, and hideous intentions of people in power.

Such fabricated accusations as "heresy," which is a belief or opinion contrary to orthodox Christian religious doctrine, became offenses punishable by death. And any opposite opinion by anyone could be labelled as heresy. Christian religious principles were compromised and sometimes abandoned to pave the way for the economic and political fortunes of leaders.

Massive exploitation of land, environment, and people was encouraged by the state and Church in the quest to acquire wealth to build empires stretching to all corners of the globe.

Abominable practices, such as the shameful buying and selling of humans as slaves, were openly conducted in towns and cities across Europe and in faraway places where they had established their outposts and type of governance.

Wars were fought in faraway lands over the natural resources belonging to other people and over the economic profits to be obtained in these places. Sometimes, when the wars were lost, rivers and wells were deliberately poisoned and the earth scorched in retribution, to the detriment of the environment and the indigenous peoples.

Mutilation and genocide were carried out with impunity in many continents in order to suppress any form of resistance from the local people, and the history, cultures, and traditions of natives were distorted, and in many cases permanently erased.

While all these shameful and un-Christian acts were going on in Europe and within the European empires, the Church looked the other way, and in certain cases willingly chose to support the state in their ruthless quest for wealth, power, and the exploitation of people and the environment—with no regard for the will of God. And all of these were swept under the pretentious carpet of civilization or simply glossed over and passed on to the next generation of rulers, who continued with the same intention but on an ever-increasing global scale.

I would conclude by saying that sometimes the injustices of man against man are too much to bear and too painful to contemplate.

As we consider the evidence against human rulers, it would be wise to note the recurring pattern of mistakes, injustice, cruelty, mismanagement, and incompetence, dating as far back as the beginning of recorded history, knowing that it will never get better. Just as it happened in Europe in the medieval period, so also it was happening in other parts of the world.

Let us take another example.

AFRICA

There were several monarchies in Africa during the medieval era and the period that followed thereafter, and some of them continue to exist in our present time. Many of them operated as self-governing states, territories, and nations, while a few thrived as kingdoms.

The majority of the African monarchs ruled in the same way as kings do all over the world, in a pattern where supreme power resides with an individual recognized as the head of state or the man on top. Most of them are similar to one another in that the sovereign inherits his office and will do anything possible to keep it until his death or until his abdication.

Many of these rulers were kings, and in certain cases, a few were queens. In order to exercise their power, the monarchs in Africa created superiority myths through rituals and symbolism laced with practices that were intended to encourage their subjects to see and regard them as mediators between the gods and the people. They elevated themselves to a privileged position above the common people, pretending to show benevolence and compassion for the people they represented and projecting the facade that their interests were above favoritism and prejudices—as if their leadership were charitable rather than for profit and personal enrichment.

Many of these kingdoms relied on taxation of local goods, such as handicrafts and intertribal trade articles, whose merchants were taxed to fill the coffers of the king. Tributes were received from various tributary chiefdoms and enclaves on the periphery of the kingdom in order to support their economy.

However, with the advent of Arabic-Islamic traders and visitors across the Sahara from the north—and the Christian European traders who came in from the west and south with their ships—a new kind of trade developed across Africa that left a devastating and disastrous aftermath in the kingdoms of Africa, as never seen before. This was the slave trade, and its impact was felt across all levels of African societies. Before this time, many kings and leaders acquired captives as a result of military and political conflicts, but very few of them pursued slave trading for profit, as it was regarded as an abomination.

During this period, many kingdoms were based on ethnic groups, and ethnic identities were very influential. Because of this, these groups did not share a common African identity, but instead identified cultural and ethnic differences, such as Ashanti, Mende, Yoruba, Igbo, Hausa and Fulani etc., as social divisions.

The frequent conflicts between these groups produced captives who could circulate in the local slave-trade system. But when the Arabs and Europeans arrived on the scene, these captives ended up in servitude to the foreigners and eventually in the trans-Atlantic and trans-Saharan slave-trade systems.

So, observing that humans were exchanged for servitude in these places, Europeans took advantage of a preexisting slave-exchange system in Africa and transformed it into an international trade to obtain labor for the expanding plantation economies of the Caribbean and North and South America.

In order to expand this trade, the Europeans went to great lengths to influence African kings and leaders to provide enslaved Africans for the trans-Atlantic slave trade. They encouraged African consumer demands for European products such as firearms, gun powder, muskets, and whiskey. And they formed military alliances to instigate fighting and increase the number of captives.

Because of these alliances, many states based on slavery grew in power and influence. For example, the Kingdom of Dahomey became one of the most prosperous nations in West Africa during this period.

But the impact of this trade in those early days was only to increase the fortunes of individual kings in the short run, because through their absurd competition with each other, many rulers of this period inadvertently engaged in a sinister trade with Europeans that had their powers reduced or eliminated entirely.

Due to the roles played by kings, chiefs, warlords, middlemen, traders, and merchants, the human loss and the disruptive effects on the social, political, military, and labor systems caused by the slave trade have been devastating to Africans and black people all over the world.

In the long run, the scale and scope of the slave trade is largely responsible for the following conditions that carry on even into the twenty-first-century world of today.

- Instability and collapse in many African states and kingdoms.
- Constrained economic development of African states.
- Ethnic and social divisions among African people.
- A culture of political violence and disregard for human life.
- Widespread attitudes of racism against black people and contempt for Africans in general.

Sadly, the damage of this era is seen in an ignorant perception in the minds of many people who justify their continued discrimination and perpetration of hate against peoples of African descent.

ASIA

Remarkably, it is not just another fleeting happenstance that throughout time, there has been no shortage of rulers who have ruled others to their own detriment, from Europe to Africa and all the way into the historic empires of Asia. And one of the most well-known Asian leaders in history is none other than Genghis Khan.

His real name was Temujin, and he was born into a noble clan in Mongolia. However, through sheer willpower, craftiness, brutality, and ruthlessness, he founded and established the Mongolian Empire. In a span of twenty-five years, his army of bloodthirsty horsemen conquered an area of land many times greater than the Roman Empire.

Due to Genghis Khan's military exploits and bloodthirstiness, the millions of people conquered by his army referred to him as evil incarnate. In Mongolia and Central Asia, however, he was widely revered because he established trade routes and promoted religious tolerance within his empire.

Moreover, Genghis Khan inaugurated the adoption of a record-keeping writing system, conducted a regular census, and introduced the first international postal system. He was also known to have fathered several thousands of people across Asia, because of his insatiable appetite for women.

At the same time, he committed despicable crimes against humanity, and millions of people died during his wars. This is mainly because soldiers, captives, and ordinary people were often used as human shields as a carefully planned tactic to spread terror and enhance his vicious image.

Genghis Khan was an enigmatic leader who chose to be open to all religions because he understood the significance and insights different religions possessed. He realized that through them, he could educate and control the people of his empire under his banner. Even up till this present time, many would argue that he is the reason that Buddhism spread all over Asia.

Despite his religious tolerance and social policies, which supported and promoted women's rights, history will remember him always as one of the most vicious tyrants, who carried out genocide whose losses number in the millions. Among genocides carried out by leaders, his are still regarded as one of a kind.

Nevertheless, there has never been a shortage of bad rulers, and there are many examples of rulers who committed serious atrocities and wicked acts of genocide in their times. Some of them are still regarded as the worst rulers in history.

Famous among them are Tamerlane or Timur, the Turkic conqueror who used barbarism to establish the Timurid dynasty; King Leopold of Belgium, who exterminated more than twelve million Congolese people in order to extract timber, rubber, and ivory from the Congo region in Africa; and last but not least, Adolf Hitler, who killed more than six million Jews and plunged the whole world into the mayhem of the Second World War.

Some of these rulers were so bad and their pattern of reasoning so terribly flawed that many harsh things have been written about them. What really defined them was that they had great power, but they chose not to use it for the betterment of humanity.

If you look beyond Genghis Khan of Asia and the other aforementioned leaders, you will notice that even in China, Japan, Persia, the rest of Asia, and North and South America, there has been no human ruler who has been able to show all the qualities that make a great leader.

Some of these qualities are as follows:

- FEAR OF GOD. A great leader must recognize there is a power above and accept that this power is absolute.
- WISDOM. A great leader must know how to discern right from wrong and must know how to make the right decisions.
- COMPASSION. A great leader must understand what his people are going through so as to be attuned to the sufferings

of the common people. He must not be arrogant but be gentle in his efforts to uplift those who are suffering.

- SELFLESS SERVICE TO THE PEOPLE. A great leader must consider the people first before making any decision.
- HUMILITY. A great leader must admit his mistakes and learn from them in order to avoid making them again. He must elevate those around him through example.
- HONESTY. A great leader must uphold truth and integrity, and he must maintain the trust and confidence given to him by the people, as well as not embezzling the funds of his nation.
- RESPECT. A great leader must respect the constitution of his country. He must abide by the laws and honor the decisions of the supreme court of his land. He must also listen to and respect the views of the common people who voted him into office. He must never imagine himself to be above the law.
- COURAGE. A great leader must have the courage to carry out the decisions that are right for the nation. He must be unafraid to stand and fight for righteousness for the sake of his people.
- INDEPENDENCE. A great leader must be strong. He must not be a puppet, and his actions must not be based on the influence of those around him. He must not be manipulated by other leaders or oligarchs, billionaires, warlords, or a few people who are thirsty for power and the wealth of the nation.
- JUSTICE. A great leader must understand that everyone is equal under the law—including both him and his inner circle—and he must understand more than everybody else that justice delayed is justice denied.

- LOVE. A great leader must have real love for his people, because of all the qualities that he must possess, it is real love that can bind them all.

In the next chapter, the spotlight will be on the modern rulers of our time, including kings, presidents, prime ministers, chancellors, and other heads of governments. Their actions will be considered in order to find out if there is any evidence to suggest that their rulership will bring about the much-needed relief for mankind as explained by Albert Einstein, who suggested many years ago that "we shall require a substantially new manner of thinking if mankind is to survive." If you consider the worsening situation of things around the world, I would say that Einstein's suggestion has more than a grain of truth in it. But there are many among us who think that knowledge and technology will solve these problems. Some of them in leadership positions believe that what is lacking is the global consciousness and the will to execute it. Therefore, they have concluded that knowledge is not lacking— rather, execution is.

In contrast to this opinion, I am writing this book to provide evidence that despite modern technology, great achievements of mankind, and the stupendous amount of knowledge and wealth available to governments, organizations, and individuals, humanity still needs divine intervention to fix the sorry situation in the world today. A corrupt foundation can never be used to build lasting sustainability.

Nevertheless, I would like to remind you that the Scriptures foretold that mankind would face harsh, difficult, and critical conditions. The

Bible also promised a rulership that would provide the much-needed solution for humanity. Let us look to the future with that in mind. The Bible assures us in Isaiah 65:16–17:

> So that he who blesses himself in the earth
> shall bless himself in the God of truth;
> and he who swears in the earth
> shall swear by the God of truth;
> because the former troubles are forgotten,
> And because they are hidden from My eyes.
> For behold, I create new heavens and a new earth;
> And the former shall not be remembered or come to mind.

For this reason, therefore, the question to ask is, whom do we trust? God, or man? We will find out soon enough when we consider the ways of modern kings.

CHAPTER SEVEN

MODERN KINGS

I n our world today, it would be easy to be subtly misled into thinking that everything is going to be alright and normal. But before you do that, ask yourself, what is *alright*, what is *normal*, and what do *alright* and *normal* look like? They look like Poverty, insecurity, pestilence, pollution, global warming, and refugee crises?

I confess that my generation does not know what *alright* is or what *normal* means. I can only imagine them and what they are supposed to look like. All I know is that millions of people go to bed hungry every day, and more than two billion people on earth live in poverty. To me, that is not alright, and neither is it normal.

I assume that as you are reading this book, you are aware that many people, including women and children, are suffering and dying in many countries because they are caught up in wars and conflicts they did not start and wars that have nothing to do with them. This is not alright and certainly not normal.

It is also a cause for concern that due to human activities, pandemic outbreaks have come to be regarded as an ever-present reality of life. Despite the efforts of leading scientists around the world and despite the huge scientific and medical advances, the potential for diseases to spread today is constantly increasing.

The massive increase in globalization and connectivity has resulted in the spread of viruses from one side of the world to another in just a few hours. That is why we have witnessed in recent decades the overwhelming effects of such diseases as HIV/AIDS, SARS, Ebola, and COVID-19. If this is normal, then normal is very scary.

It is generally acknowledged by scientists, organizations, and even the United Nations Food and Agriculture Organization that the natural resources of our planet, including its forests, marine life, wild animals, and crop lands, are already overexploited at an unsustainable rate.[23]

Many people all over the world are witnessing the gradual increase in the extinction of species and the destruction of natural habitats, like the tropical rain forest, whole ocean ecosystems, and the depletion of the earth's biosphere.

It is certain that things will never be alright if concrete action is not taken by leaders and policy makers while human population continues to grow, and the increasingly unsustainable economic practices continue to impose pressure on the earth's ecosystem.

With a growing world population of more than seven billion people, the planet is struggling to cope with the demands placed upon it by humans. When you add the human factor of greed and avarice, then we are headed toward the point of no return. This means that in the near future, there will be scarcity of resources, food shortages, and food-price hikes that will be the new normal and the shape of things to come.

---

[23] "The Change of Sustainability," Food and Agriculture Organization of the United Nations, fao.org/3/u8480e/U8480E0z.htm.

Global warming is another major problem that is already upon mankind, and its effect can now be felt on every part of the globe. There was a time when it could have been argued endlessly whether global warming is man-made or a naturally occurring anomaly. However, there is scientific evidence to show that global warming is indeed upon us, and it is caused by human activities. It is apparent that uncontrolled human activities have increased the melting of glaciers and polar ice. There are also substantial changes in rainfall patterns and actual increases in measured surface temperatures in different regions of the world. Because of this, it is projected by the scientific community that if serious action is not taken, global warming will continue, with potentially dire consequences for vast numbers of people living on this planet.

I would state in a clear and certain way that it is not alright and absolutely not normal that due to our own actions, we are already being affected by climate change in a way that is detrimental to human life and well-being. It is estimated that at least thirty thousand people died as a direct result of the 2003 heat wave that was felt over Western Europe, and many of the dead were the very old and the very young.

Another indirect consequence of climate change is Hurricane Katrina, which hit the Southern coastal city of New Orleans in the USA a few years ago and is estimated to have killed over 1,800 people. Global warming is also associated with the deaths of millions of people in developing countries as a result of crop failures caused by droughts. This could be a constant scenario of the near future.

These problems mentioned above and many others, such as severe water shortages, corruption, immorality, global terrorism, universal decline of true religion, tyranny, and the pollution of space above the earth, give us a chance to observe how modern kings—that is, presidents, prime ministers, chancellors, and other global leaders—are thinking about solving our most pressing problems. Please be aware that I am using the term *modern kings* to refer to all the people in power and at the very top of decision making in various countries of the world.

At the time of this writing, these leaders and their representatives, supported by the corporate social movers and shakers, will soon be meeting in Davos, Switzerland, where they assemble every year for the annual meeting of the World Economic Forum. They will pledge to commit hundreds of millions of dollars to public and private partnerships that address the world's most urgent challenges, notably:

- Climate change
- Poverty and corruption
- Pandemics and chronic diseases
- Illiteracy, plastic waste in the oceans, and much more

Unfortunately, after the initial fanfare and glitzy public announcements, most of these sincere and well-intentioned global initiatives are almost certain to fail because there is no accountability and no obligation to answer to anyone.

The idea of governments and global corporations partnering together to foster social progress is not wrong. Rather, the question is how they can do so in a way that realistically achieves social impact and delivers actual value to the needs of people.

Ironically, these partnerships rarely solve these problems. Instead, they collapse under their own weight and become broken, as those involved become discouraged by the lack of meaningful progress for society, or lack of economic benefit for the shareholders of the corporations involved.

This situation can be avoided if the partnerships of governments and corporations will adopt a clear strategy of who will be responsible for where, when, and how to develop solutions, and if they will form coalitions that can advance progress on specific issues in a particular region, connecting closely to the businesses and local needs of those in that region.

This means that local solutions are the mechanism to tackle global problems, for in this manner, responsibility is placed on the designated governments, organizations, and leaders. If they don't deliver, they can be held accountable, and if there is proof of embezzlement, they can be prosecuted to the last penny.

All over the world, there is money to be made by meeting the world's challenges. In fact, billions of dollars can be made from new business opportunities. On the other hand, money and lives will be lost by not tackling the challenges, because calamitous societal failures, business failures, and failure in educational systems will result from inaction.

In appreciation of the initiatives of the World Economic Forum, I would recommend that leaders recognize that there are opportunities in every region of the world. Therefore, they have to figure out how to meaningfully collaborate with governments in these regions, NGOs, relevant local chieftains, and local populations to create the systemic change that the world wants to achieve. Where this method of collaboration is already in existence, it should be widely encouraged to flourish.

Moreover, I believe that when governments and organizations are encouraged to work openly in this way, with nothing to hide and no ulterior motives of domination, many companies and corporations will join them to generate value for the society and value for their shareholders.

This can be a better way of tackling these challenges, and it might serve as a workable platform to support the "normal" that current generations are hoping to see but are yet to experience in different regions of the world.

However, for many people to experience relative normality, our leaders have to find a way to tackle one of the most serious challenges of the present day—this is the issue of corruption in high places. It is on the minds of most people, yet there is no organized will from the top to fight it.

CORRUPTION

It may be convenient *not* to talk about corruption because of the assumption that a vast majority of people are involved in it. But if many at the top are willingly engaging in corruption, then it becomes necessary to point out that it looms over the world, creating problems for communities across the globe. It is growing and spreading rapidly like cancer cells all over the world, and it is threatening to destroy the collective credibility and trust in leaders, organizations, financial institutions, judicial institutions, and governments. Corruption is everywhere, from developing nations to developed countries.

The scourge of corruption involves leaders of countries, public officials, business managers, and private citizens who engage in the illegal acts of bribery, money laundering, embezzlement of public funds, and lobbying, boosted by trading and peddling in influence of quid pro quo—the most elevated form of corruption being practiced by people in high places.

In the past, the general perception was that corruption was a problem that mostly effects developing nations, but—on the contrary—it has been revealed that corruption is embedded in the private and public institutions of developed countries as well.

For instance, there are scandalous examples of leaders who facilitate money-laundering activities through state-owned banks, leaders who are involved in tax evasion, and leaders who steal billions of dollars from their national coffers and from election-campaign funds raised from donors. There are also modern-day presidents and other national leaders in power who receive hefty bribes and connive with multinationals to secure lucrative public contracts.

There is also petty corruption that does not make headlines, nonetheless its cost is arguably greater than that of large-scale corruption. It might be happening in the form of favors—in small amounts of pounds, euros, and dollars that add up precipitously—and it is happening right now all over the world.

However, in whatever form it is happening, corruption causes poverty, delays development, and drives away investment. It weakens the political and judicial systems that should be working for the public good and erodes trust in government officials and national institutions.

Moreover, corruption ensures that many people are left behind, marginalized, and far worse off, thereby facilitating human trafficking, terrorism, and organized crime.

Sadly, many leaders are expected to fight corruption. But on the contrary, they seek public office with the sole intention of enriching themselves and those around them, thereby entrenching corruption in government institutions and using these institutions to persecute those who dare to challenge them.

IMMORALITY

Without any doubt, there are acts by groups and individuals all over the world that go against accepted conduct, norms, decency, and standards of human dignity. To give the benefit of the doubt, many human behaviors might be contrary to established standards of morality and may differ according to race, culture, and creed. Moreover, from time to time, from one generation to another and from place to place, norms are bound to differ.

Some of these norms may include acts of violence, sexual misconduct, behaviors we might consider perverse, unreasonable, and unacceptable, and such afflictions as alcoholism and drug addiction. Notwithstanding that all of the above are immoral acts, I would rather focus on the major problems of immorality happening on a global scale in many countries and condemned generally by people from most walks of life. Some of these immoral acts include:

- Dehumanization
- Human trafficking

- Slavery
- Trading in human body parts
- Development and manufacture of deadly nerve agents and biological weapons
- Cloning of humans and other species
- Unethical killing and sanctioned execution of critics and perceived enemies by powerful leaders

It is wrong to assume that because the modern world is unable to put forward a coherent definition of morality, that these acts will be tolerated or accepted by the vast majority of people worldwide, for even those who do not trust religion or believe in God are vehemently against these inhuman practices.

It is disheartening to note that many have refused to use the wonderful gift of free will from God as a moral compass to choose between right and wrong, and this has led to the popular attitude that everything is permitted. This attitude is not only found in the general population but also among modern leaders of our time as well. And because of this line of thinking, there is an unprecedented rise in mental and spiritual problems causing people to do things that are detrimental to their own well-being and the well-being of others.

A major sign of our time is a falling away from religion, an increased tendency toward atheism, and large numbers of people who do not believe in God yet are in a constant state of swinging one way or the other regarding what they believe. So, in various parts of the world, there is a steady decrease in the numbers of people who would consider themselves religious in any sense of the word.

Because of this modern condition, many are now confronted by uncertainty, immorality, meaninglessness, doubt of traditional values, and overwhelming feelings of helplessness and malaise. And this condition is further compounded by addiction to social media, sensational news shows, and binge television laced with immoral content.

However, it would be wrong to allow technological advancement and scientific rationalism of the modern age to manipulate us to abandon many of the beliefs that make life meaningful, because these beliefs, when placed in a religious context, give a sense of purpose, security, and comfort.

It would be wise to remember that while science and technology have given humanity a cold and sterile clockwork knowledge of the earth and universe, a scientific worldview devoid of spiritual purpose, and ultimate theories with no room for traditional ideas about God, nothing satisfactory has come along to replace the loving Creator who designed and created humans and all that we know as the universe today.

This may seem like the sort of topic people would prefer to think of as personal—to believe in religion and God or not to believe—but clinical and scientific study after study has shown the power of religion to help people cope with moral issues, stress, and adversity.

On that note, I would suggest to all modern leaders that they lead by the example of keeping a high moral standard based on religious principles, or the knowledge of God, so the ruled can observe and copy, because the Scriptures say: "Where there is no vision, the people perish: but he that keepeth the law, happy is he."[24]

---

[24]   Proverbs 29:18 KJV.

TYRANNY AND SUPPRESSION OF DEMOCRATIC VALUES

In this modern world, it might be preposterous to suggest that entire populations of countries are brought under the control of a tiny self-serving minority at the expense of individual freedoms and the greater good of the majority, but that may be so. Only time will tell.

We know that in many regions of the world, the modern economic system has created a model whereby the rich tend to get even richer and further consolidate their economic power through acquisition of political power by financial means. It is now normal to say that political power is acquired through financial power and used for more financial gain.

Shamelessly, without any remorse from the individuals involved, this pattern of using economic power to acquire political power is carried out brazenly right in our face, making it obvious for all to see, both in democratic countries and undemocratic nations.

The more you observe this trend, the more it appears that the world is heading toward a corrupt one-world tyranny, controlled by less than 10 percent of the entire world population, who may one day have total control over the political, economic, judicial, law enforcement, and military institutions of the whole world.

This may seem like the stuff of far-fetched conspiracy theories. Nonetheless, the entire world is bearing witness to examples of leaders who have appropriated state institutions to ensure that they remain unchallenged in power. Some leaders have even gone to the extremes of developing deadly nerve agents, which they use to poison and silence political opponents both at home and abroad.

There are now leaders who misuse their countries' property abroad to literally dismember critics and dispose of their bodies in parts, in a gruesome and undiplomatic manner, with no regard for decency and the rule of international law. Many leaders are also known to have used diplomatic buildings to carry out torture and unlawful interrogations in foreign countries.

Yet, a few of our modern leaders consider themselves clever because they foment conflicts, sow divisions, and start wars during election seasons or during the handing over of power in order to remain in charge, with no regard for the suffering and deaths of helpless men, women, and children sacrificed for their inordinate power plays.

It may seem incongruous that even in these modern times characterized by state-of the-art technology, abundant know-how, premium quality education, stupendous wealth, and new ideas, we have leaders who want to turn back the hands of the clock to feudal times and a medieval way of ruling while still taking advantage of the modern system of things.

In some countries, leaders and politicians are resorting to divide-and-conquer tactics and stoking of racial sentiments, including demonization of helpless refugees and manipulation of news media, to perpetuate their stranglehold on power. If you are paying close attention, you will notice that they have transformed real news based on facts into fake news such that fake news based on lies has taken the place of real news.

And for many leaders of our time, shameless is the new normal and alternate reality is the new reality—especially in the advanced democratic countries of the world. For instance, instead of upholding democratic principles and formulating policies that will improve the welfare of their citizens, their first order of business is to change the very election laws that brought them to power and craft new laws that will make it very difficult for people to vote, thereby eliminating popular vote and allowing only sympathetic votes that will ensure their continuous grip on power. As if this undemocratic ploy were not shameful enough, they even engage corrupt individuals with impeccable knowledge of the law to cajole and force foreign nations to help them win local and national elections by fabricating lies disguised as truth overseas.

Some of these elected leaders have even gone to the extent of manipulating the Christian evangelical movement in order to achieve political gain. They have succeeded in splitting and sowing divisions in the ranks of this popular Christian demographic into two opposing factions of white evangelicals and black evangelicals, thereby making a mockery of the well-meaning intention of religious support for a healthy political environment.

Furthermore, they instigate and sponsor extremist fringe elements of the society and home-grown terrorists to threaten and harass other politicians who refuse to see things their way. Lawlessness, violent insurrections, and storming of legislative institutions are not ruled out in order to make sure that their one-sided interpretation of governance is forced down the throat of the majority.

This unending trend of bad rulership is fully on display all over the world, and sometimes it seems one leader is trying to outdo the other. Because of this attitude, it would not be wrong to assume that many leaders today consider human rights and good governance as overrated ideas.

It is now imperative that people all over the world cry out that this caricature of leadership is not what governance is all about. Even as you are reading this book, I would humbly remind you that more than one million people from the northwestern region of a certain country are currently being detained in what a leader defines as "reeducation" camps, where they are being used as forced labor and the women are forcibly sterilized—just because they happen to be Muslim.

Reporters and journalists who dare to report these atrocities are killed indiscriminately, and democracy and human-rights activists are harassed, jailed, and forced to flee their countries of birth. Even recently, an F-16 fighter jet was used to force a public aircraft flying over the international airspace of a European nation to land in the capital, and a critic of the president was abducted from the plane and subsequently tortured with impunity, with no respect for international law and in total disregard for the human rights of all the passengers on that aircraft.

With this type of autocratic mindset and strong-man mentality of some leaders in different regions of the world, we are also seeing other leaders in some democratic countries who are now testing the waters to see how far they can go in chipping away the democratic principles that serve as check and balance in the system of democracy.

For example, they no longer honor international treaties and agreements drafted to ensure peace and prosperity in their regions. Some leaders lobby and successfully block motions presented by the United Nations to curtail their unilateral ambitions and high-handedness in dealing with situations in their respective regions of the world. In fact, democratic nations are arguably the ones undermining the credibility of the United Nations, and they are getting away with it.

From what we are witnessing in the twenty-first century, it seems this is the right time to remember that way back in 1947, Winston Churchill said that "democracy is the worst form of government, except for all those other forms that have been tried." However, if the type of democracy on display now on the international stage is the model to which nations should aspire, then the ideals of the democratic system of government have been rendered ineffective and dumped into the free-for-all theatre of those who are willing to shout the most.

Furthermore, as this model continues to spread all over the globe, even diehard believers in democratic government are beginning to realize that the myth surrounding government of the people, by the people, and for the people, which has sustained democracy over the years, has been totally broken and emasculated.

Even George Orwell recognized the slippery descent of modern politics into lies, half-truths, and machinations. Therefore, he cautioned in *1984*, "Political language is designed to make lies sound truthful and murder respectable."[25] It would be correct to say that many modern-day politicians have adopted this statement as their modus operandi.

While this trend might appear innocuous and hazy, it would be wise to be alert and well informed to understand that for tyranny to rise, all democratic principles must be dismantled and weakened, and the will of the people must be broken slowly and steadily to set the stage for a tyrannical rude awakening.

---

[25] George Orwell, *1984* (London: Martin Secker & Warburg Ltd., 1949). Many editions available.

Furthermore, before tyranny is unleashed, the perception of the people must be manipulated in such a way that they will not understand the real intention of the reality foisted upon them. It has happened before, and it might happen again.

After observing and considering the above-mentioned facts about modern leaders, we must remember that the economic and political advantage they gain through unscrupulous and devious means has to be kept secret from the wider public by enlisting the support of secret societies that serve the interest of its faceless members. I have no other option than to conclude that the evil and self-serving world tyranny might imminently be upon mankind.

SPACE EXPLORATION AND POLLUTION

Over the years, the moon landings and space exploration have been presented to the wider public with much fanfare and extensive television coverage in such a way that portrays them as exciting and profitable.

However, what are never discussed are the potential dangers, expenses, and pollution that space exploration would bring us as well. Therefore, as we celebrate the successful accomplishments of going to space and back, it is also necessary to examine the advantages and disadvantages of space exploration before launching these missions to ensure that the best possible result for mankind is achieved.

The advantages of space exploration include the following:

- Many would argue that space exploration allows us to prepare for potential future hazards, especially if you consider that in our solar system alone, asteroids and comets could devastate our planet if an impact were to occur. Therefore, exploring space gives us an early-warning opportunity to locate these hazards and to prepare for an encounter to help preserve mankind.

- Through space exploration, we can discover new things about our planet and maybe new life and cultures simultaneously.

- Travelling to space requires innovation, so the human effort to solve critical space problems can create opportunities to make life better here on earth. Technologies that were originally developed for space programs, such as LED-lighting, anti-icing devices, and memory foam, are now used on earth in other areas of life.

- Space exploration is one of the few human endeavors that promotes cooperation among competing nations. It can be said that despite the political disputes that occur between these nations, their capability to work together on space programs can develop into new standards for future agreements to resolve complicated issues facing humanity.

- Space exploration can be used as a platform to encourage competing leaders and governments to share instead of being selfish. It can also be used as a channel to find common ground outside our national identity, physical appearance, cultural differences, and political preferences.

However, despite the advantages that are gained from the exploration of space, there are huge prices to pay and serious risks and consequences that result from these missions. For example:

- Space exploration is an expensive project. In the last decade, the efforts of the United States of America alone cost more than $200 billion dollars. When you add the costs from other countries and their space programs, we find that on average more than $60 billion dollars per year is spent on this effort. However, by comparison, the United Nations is only asking for half of that amount annually to end global hunger permanently. So, ask yourself, should space exploration be the top priority of leaders if we are struggling to feed the poor among us here on earth?

- Exploration of space creates high-level pollution events. It takes a large quantity of fossil fuels to launch rockets into space, and this produces a significant level of pollution every time fuel is expended for exploration purposes. Larger models of space rockets can carry as much as five-hundred thousand gallons of fuel to be used during an entire mission. This means that millions of pounds of carbon pollution are released into the atmosphere with every action taken to reach space. Yet, there has been no 100 percent efficient method found to place these fossil fuels into orbit in order to make exploration endeavors emissions free. In fact, space exploration is creating even further potential contamination for our atmosphere.

- Instead of unity, space exploration is creating suspicion, mistrust, and needless competition among leaders involved in this project. The original goal was to make reaching the stars a great accomplishment for humanity so that no one could claim a territory in orbit or a territory of our solar system that could give one nation a distinct advantage over others, because it was understood that space belongs to all of mankind.

However, the journey to space has turned into a rat-race such that some leaders with unrestrained ambition to dominate others have decided to come up with the idea of creating a space force that could be used to upset the balance that leaders before them worked hard to establish and maintain over the last fifty years. These leaders are no longer satisfied with spying on each other by using satellites to monitor one another's communication networks or even hacking one another's computer infrastructure. Rather, they want to take it to the next level of potentially targeting cities with weapons from their spacecraft high above the earth. Sure enough, this paranoia will continue to multiply as humans' push further into the stars.

- At the time of the writing of this book, NASA is tracking more than a half million pieces of space junk circling our planet. With no proven human technology yet to physically remove these items, this garbage will linger and proceed to break up into smaller pieces until it falls into our atmosphere to burn up and create more pollution problems for the air quality that we breathe. Now that many countries and wealthy individuals are involved in space exploration, it would be wise for them to consider that every item left behind creates a future risk of space pollution. Therefore, before anyone starts to explore space, they must also look for ways to clean up the mess they are sure to leave behind. It is bad enough that humans have polluted the oceans with chemicals and plastics—it will be disastrous if we do the same above us.

Therefore, before undertaking future missions to space, we must ask ourselves if there are valid reasons to begin this effort or if it is only for pride and braggadocio. Because from what we have witnessed so far, the truth is that there are few pragmatic benefits from this endeavor.

On the other hand, since we are still dealing with serious issues like crime, poverty, epidemics, refugee crises, and pollution here on earth, addressing mankind's immediate concerns might be better than looking at future fancy needs that might never come to pass.

Now that we have considered some of the major issues facing humanity today, it is time to urge our leaders to come up with ideas and possible solutions to tackle these problems, because it seems as if time and hope are running out for humans to turn things around.

THE HIGH IDEALS OF HUMAN LEADERSHIP

I would hereby remind every modern king, queen, or president—including prime ministers, chancellors, or even premiers and dictators—that a leader must be a dealer in hope. They are neither inventors nor explorers, and a majority of them are not scientists or innovators. Rather, they are in their positions because of their eloquent mastery of words and their ability to somehow convince people to elect them to serve, or in some cases to have them as monarchs.

Therefore, if scientists, inventors, developers, innovators, and doctors have contributed to creating the modern world as we know it today, the least any modern king can do is to give hope that the modern technology and advancements can be used to make things better in a world where millions of people are hopeless. These leaders should be grateful for the abundant availability of funds, technology, and know-how at this time in human history. All they have to do is to harness these advantages and use them to create a better world.

It is time to discard the old ways of reasoning and doing things by pitting people against each other, because it does not work, has never worked, and has only succeeded in creating a distorted way of life in our current system of things.

Our system is characterized by double-speak and covering up all forms of despicable and immoral acts against humanity and against God, and it keeps piling up over the centuries. These acts were mostly committed by the high-and-mighty human rulers who should know better and have remained mostly covered up and uncorrected up until the present time.

It is a well-known fact that nothing goes for nothing. Therefore, the present style of divide and rule and divide and conquer must stop, along with the politics of bombast and vanity. If politics is the most popular path to becoming a ruler, then leaders should stop promising that they will do something good if elected without following through after the elections. They must have the guts to say they are only interested in enriching themselves and then see what the electorate thinks of them.

Indeed, our modern rulers need to be constantly reminded to:

- Be kind.
- Be fair.
- Be honest.
- Be truthful.

Of course, they know that all these things are expected of them. People all over the world want to see these attributes in their leaders in order to rekindle the hope that things will be alright.

People all over the world are also becoming weary of constantly reminding our current leaders that they should be familiar with the great achievements of leaders in the past who had a vision for a better world and made sure that it was accepted. One important achievement that gave hope to billions of people was the United Nations' adoption of the Universal Declaration of Human Rights. It was an awesome relief to many people that, after centuries of religious persecution, widespread injustice, and gross disregard for human rights, the Declaration was universally recognized. Even in our present time, it is regarded as one of the great achievements of modern history.

The respect for human rights was so important that Thomas Jefferson enshrined it into the United States Constitution so that America would be a nation that honors human rights at all levels of government. Jefferson wrote that:

> We hold these truths to be self-evident, that all men are created equal, that they are endowed by their Creator with certain unalienable rights, that among these are Life, Liberty and the pursuit of Happiness.

The US Declaration of Independence is still there for all to see, as it has been since July 4, 1776.[26]

---

[26] "Declaration of Independence," July 4, 1776, National Archives, archives. gov/founding-docs/declaration-transcript.

Another leader realized the value and importance of human rights and decided to make it a fundamental document of the French Revolution. General Lafayette was so influenced by Jefferson's notion that he introduced it as Article 1 of the document of the French Revolution. It states:

Men are born and remain free and equal in rights. Social distinctions can be founded only upon the general good.[27]

However, if any modern king or leader or president or prime minister or chancellor decides not to uphold the rights of his people in any way whatsoever, I would like to remind him or her that in the twentieth century, the United Nations Universal Declaration of Human Rights cemented the importance of those rights for modern history. It was adopted by the UN Security Council on December 10, 1948, and it begins with the following assumption:

> Whereas recognition of the inherent dignity and of the equal and inalienable rights of all members of the human family is the foundation of freedom, justice and peace in the world.

This declaration is the foundation of democracy, and democracy gives everyone the right to participate in how they are governed. That is why democracy was defined by Abraham Lincoln, borrowing from words written centuries earlier by John Wycliffe, as "government of the people, by the people and for the people."[28]

---

[27]   "Declaration of the Rights of Man," August 26, 1789, Avalon Project at Yale Law School, avalon.law.yale.edu/18th_century/rightsof.asp.

[28]   Gabor S. Boritt, ed., *Of the People, By the People, For the People* (New York: Columbia University Press, 1996), xiv.

If so, then ask yourself, why are so few benefitting from "government of the people"? Why is it that in most democratic countries of the world, only about 1 percent of the total population can pick up the telephone and talk to their president or vice-president or have a say in the decision-making process concerning themselves? Why are the conditions of living becoming more and more difficult for many people, despite the fact that the government should be "for the people"—especially when you consider that the majority of the citizenry does not have access to their leaders, and these leaders live in extravagant opulence while the people pay all sorts of taxes to carry the burden of their countries over the top-heavy governments?

When you consider all of this, is there any sign that our modern leaders can suddenly or gradually turn things around and create a situation that will be regarded by all as normal? Or are we expecting too much from humans just like ourselves?

Maybe it's time to look beyond our present reality and our expectations to understand that there is another way available. It is possible to achieve the true meaning of the words, "All men are created equal, that they are endowed by their Creator with certain unalienable rights, that among these are Life, Liberty and the pursuit of Happiness."

I am saying this because during my research on the origins of the difficulties in our present system of things, I realized many leaders in the past and the present do not possess the capability or the knowledge necessary to eradicate all these problems.

Therefore, no one is to be blamed for our present predicament, as even the writers of the Scriptures recognized. That is why

Jeremiah wrote in the Bible, in Jeremiah 10:23: "O LORD, I know the way of man is not in himself; it is not in man who walks to direct his steps."

This does not mean that there is no hope for a better future for mankind. Rather, it means we should be looking beyond our present leaders and be prepared to welcome a true leader—a man of the people, a King of kings foretold in the Bible who will provide solutions to all the problems currently faced by mankind.

Amid today's challenges, there is a promise that gives hope for a better future. This promise was foretold in the Bible several thousands of years ago to warn humanity of the pitfalls of human rulership and to encourage humanity. God has put in place a rescue plan to bring an end to human suffering, which is the fallout from all human leadership. This promise will unfold as a future system of things on earth, described in the Bible as the "New Jerusalem." In Isaiah 65:18–25, the Scriptures inform us about a promise from God to all people, for which we can be glad and rejoice forever. God says:

> For behold, I create Jerusalem [or a new world] as a rejoicing, and her people a joy. I will rejoice in Jerusalem, and joy in My people; the voice of weeping shall no longer be heard in her, nor the voice of crying.

Further, God promises that:

> No more shall an infant from there live but a few days, nor an old man who has not fulfilled his days; for the one who dies at a hundred will be thought a mere child; The one who fails to reach a hundred will be considered accursed.

In this new world, God says that people will build houses and dwell in them. They will plant their own vineyards and eat their fruit. They will no longer build houses that others live in, or plant crops that others eat.

> For as the days of a tree, so shall be the days of My people, and My elect shall long enjoy the work of their hands.

Moreover, in this new system of things, God reassures us that humanity will not labor in vain, nor will they bear children doomed to misfortune.

> For they shall be the descendants of the blessed of the LORD, and their offspring with them.

God continues:

> "Before they call, I will answer; and while they are still speaking, I will hear. The wolf and the lamb shall feed together, the lion shall eat straw like the ox, and dust shall be the serpent's food. They shall not hurt nor destroy in all My holy mountain," says the LORD.

In order to help humans fully comprehend the reality of this promise, the Bible paints a beautiful picture of wolves living together in peace with sheep and leopards lying down with young goats. Calves and lion cubs will feed together, and little children will be their shepherd.

Just imagine how awesome it will be to see cows and bears actually feeding together and their calves and cubs lying down in peace. Even a baby will not be harmed if it plays near a poisonous snake, and in all the earth there will be nothing harmful or evil. The whole earth will be full of the knowledge of God, just as the seas are full of water.

I am assuming that to many people this may sound like a story told in Disneyworld, or a fantasy movie too good to be true. But just as God created the earth and the universe out of nothing, He also knows best how to repair and rebuild all that He created with His own hands.

Even before all of this was foretold, God had already drawn a master plan and laid lay the foundation of this new world that He has promised to deliver to His children. Because of this, He inspired several writers in the Bible to record the details identifying the One who will make all of this possible for mankind.

God has chosen a King who will be different in His style of rulership from all other kings before Him—a ruler who will perfectly execute His plan, as well as being worthy to become the King of God's kingdom.

In the next chapter, we are going to learn everything about this Ruler, what makes Him unique and qualified to rule, and what we can expect from His government. Even in our present way of life that we are accustomed to, you should be aware that the campaign to usher in this new government has already started.

So, if you are wondering what campaign I am talking about or when it started—or if you are not yet aware of it—I would gladly inform you that even now, as you are reading this book, people are visiting other people, going door to door canvassing for this new government, while others are spreading the word through radio and television, books, and social-media outlets, bringing awareness to millions of people around the globe and urging them to choose. Only this time, every individual must decide for him or herself whether he or she wants to live in this new world promised by God.

CHAPTER EIGHT

KING JESUS

Then the angel said to her, "Do not be afraid, Mary, for you have found favor with God. And behold, you will conceive in your womb and bring forth a Son, and shall call His name JESUS. He will be great, and will be called the Son of the Highest; and the Lord God will give Him the throne of His father David.... Of His kingdom there will be no end." (Luke 1:30–33)

M any years before the birth of Jesus, the Bible foretold that God would establish a kingdom that will replace all human government and bring an end to human rule. And this kingdom will last forever. So, what is God's kingdom? And why is it a kingdom that will never end?

It is a heavenly government ruled by Jesus as King that will put an end to all bad things and bring about everlasting peace for people on earth. This kingdom is clearly foretold in the book of Isaiah, chapter 9:6–7.[29]

---

[29] Isaiah 9:6–7: "For unto us a Child is born, unto us a Son is given; and the government will be upon His shoulder. And His name will be called Wonderful, Counselor, Mighty God, Everlasting Father, Prince of Peace. Of the increase of His government and peace there will be no end, upon the throne of David and over His kingdom, to order it and establish it with judgment and justice from that time forward, even forever. The zeal of the LORD of hosts will perform this."

In order to outline why we need God's kingdom, I would like to recap that at the start of human history, God was the only ruler, and He governed in a loving way. He designed and constructed a beautiful home that He set in a paradise garden called Eden on earth for humans to live in.

He also provided food in abundance for them, and in addition, He provided meaningful work for them to do—to take care of all the animals and other creatures and to take care of the environment as well. Because of this, in hindsight, it is correct to say that mankind would have enjoyed lasting peace and prosperity if they had remained under God's loving rulership.

Of course, in the system of things then, as it was under God's rulership, all creation was united and at peace. However, something beyond the comprehension of humans happened in heaven to change the course of human history.

The Bible reveals that a rebellious angel, later known as Satan, or the devil, challenged God's right to rule. He was jealous that God loved humans so much, therefore he formulated a devious plan to convince humans they would be happier without God's direction and rulership.

He appeared in the form of a serpent and tempted our first parents, Adam and Eve, by offering them a forbidden fruit they were warned not to eat. Sadly, Adam and Eve listened to Satan and ate the fruit, rebelling against God.

This decision by Adam and Eve had consequences not only for them but for all the children they eventually had. As their descendants, we all have a nature that is inclined to reject God as our ruler, and because of this, we have lost our paradise home and the hope of living forever in perfect health on earth.

In the Scriptures, Romans 5:12 states that "sin entered the world, and death through sin." And sin is always seeking to multiply. Therefore, it led to another tragic result described in Ecclesiastes 8:9, that "man rules over another to his own hurt." In other words, Adam and Eve's sin started the chronicle of human rulership, and—as we have seen—when humans rule each other, problems are bound to happen.

This prompted King Solomon to write some three thousand years ago, "And look! The tears of the oppressed, but they have no comforter—on the side of their oppressors there is power."[30] This oppression is still going on today in our modern time, and even the United Nations has already figured this out. It stated in 2009 that "bad governance is being increasingly regarded as one of the root causes of all evil within our societies."[31]

But God, our Creator, foresaw all of this. That is why He promised to appoint a ruler who would fix all of these problems. This ruler is Jesus Christ. Certainly, the world needs a good ruler and a better form of government. That is what our Maker has promised, and that is what Jesus will deliver.

It is reassuring to learn from the Bible that God has set up a kingdom, or a new government, with a new system of doing things that will replace all human rule. This is the kingdom for which millions have been praying for, and this new kingdom will soon be inaugurated and will stand forever after inauguration.

---

[30] Ecclesiastes 4:1.
[31] "What Is Good Governance?," United Nations ESCAP, July 10, 2009, unescap.org/resources/what-good-governance.

However, God will not rule this government Himself. Instead, He chose to appoint someone who has great love for humans, has lived as a human on earth, has suffered greatly at the hands of the authorities, and understands the difficulties faced by millions of people all over the world.

And to prove beyond reasonable doubt that He appointed this ruler, God Himself declared in Psalm 2:6, 8: "I have set My King…, and I will give You the nations for Your inheritance, and the ends of the earth for Your possession."

Going further to dispel any illusion from the minds of people, God announced it formally in Micah 5:2, 4: "But you, Bethlehem Ephrata, out of you shall come forth to Me the One to be Ruler.… He shall be great to the ends of the earth."

Instead of waiting in heaven after His appointment, this Ruler chose to come to earth to understand what it means to live as a human. Despite all His efforts to show us the right way to live, He was rejected by men, and He was despised and humiliated by those in power. He was tortured and pierced for our transgressions, and many held Him as of no account, and finally, He was crushed for our errors.[32]

After He was rejected and executed by men, He was raised by God from the dead and glorified in heaven in preparation for His rulership on earth. This ruler is none other than Jesus Christ. It is important for everyone to understand that Jesus came once to the earth as Christ and Savior, but He is going to return to earth to rule as King.

In order to confirm the return of Jesus as King, the Scriptures inform mankind in the book of Revelation that: "The kingdoms of

---

[32]   Isaiah 53.

this world have become the kingdoms of our Lord and of His Christ, and He shall reign forever and ever!"[33]

Jesus has a lot on His resume that makes Him ideally qualified to rule. I would say that in all of human history, only He fits the description of an ideal ruler.

HOW WILL JESUS RULE?

Jesus will rule as King in heaven and earth, and He will be assisted by 144,000 corulers He has chosen from among mankind to be His ministers on earth.

In order to provide a clear identity of the makeup of this theocratic government, the Bible states in Revelation 14:1–3:

> Then I looked, and behold, a Lamb standing on Mount Zion, and with Him one hundred and forty-four thousand, having His Father's name written on their foreheads. And I heard a voice from heaven, like the voice of many waters, and like the voice of loud thunder. And I heard the sound of harpists playing their harps. They sang as it were a new song before the throne, before the four living creatures, and the elders; and no one could learn that song except the hundred and forty-four thousand who were redeemed from the earth.

This information from the Bible has revealed to mankind the makeup of the fundamental cabinet of this theocratic government. Notwithstanding that these cabinet members are chosen from the

---

[33] Revelation 11:15.

earth, be rest assured that Jesus has selected and vetted a well-drilled cabinet, ready and willing to carry out His instructions.

However, in order to find out how Jesus will rule the earth and what makes Him the ideal leader to lead mankind, it would be smart to consider what He did while on earth, because His way of life on earth was a preamble of what Jesus is going to bring to the table.

While on earth, Jesus performed many amazing and powerful feats to show that as a ruler, He will make things easier and much better than the life humans are living now. Jesus Christ led by example, using His healing power to cure every sort of disease, thereby demonstrating how He will eliminate sickness from mankind.

He also calmed the sea, showing how He will protect people by controlling the forces of nature. Also, as if to show that His way of life was not just about work, prayer, and preaching with no play, Jesus turned water into wine at a wedding in order to keep the party going, proving to everyone that He appreciates a groovy get-together and signifying how He will help people to enjoy life and celebrate with each other.

But, most certainly, it is a given that He has many goodies to offer and much love to distribute to humanity. For example:

JESUS WILL CARE FOR PEOPLE

Jesus was noted for His exemplary compassion for people. He helped men and women, young and old, regardless of their background and status. In comparison with His system, it is a shame that despite the abundance of resources in the world, millions of people in our present system go to bed every night hungry and thirsty, and in most cases their hunger and thirst are caused by other high-and-mighty human beings who have used them as pawns in their power struggles.

The evidence that no one will go to bed hungry was illustrated in the Bible when Jesus fed a large crowd that had come from all over the place to listen to Him. Mark 8:1–9 describes a situation where a large crowd was gathered, and it happened that the people had nothing to eat. So, Jesus called His disciples to Him and said:

> "I have compassion on the multitude, because they have now continued with Me three days and have nothing to eat. And if I send them away hungry to their own houses, they will faint on the way; for some of them have come from afar."
>
> Then His disciples answered Him, "How can one satisfy these people with bread here in the wilderness?"
>
> He asked them, "How many loaves do you have?"
>
> And they said, "Seven."
>
> So He commanded the multitude to sit down on the ground. And He took the seven loaves and gave thanks, broke them and gave them to His disciples to set before them; and they set them before the multitude. They also had a few small fish; and having blessed them, He said to set them also before them. So they ate and were filled, and they took up seven large baskets of leftover fragments. Now those who had eaten were about four thousand. And He sent them away.

This amazing feat performed by Jesus demonstrates His ability to provide food for all and eradicate hunger forever.

On another occasion, a man afflicted with leprosy came to Jesus and begged Him on his knees, saying, "'If You are willing, You can make me clean.' Then Jesus put out His hand and touched him, saying, 'I am willing; be cleansed.' Immediately his leprosy was cleansed."[34]

These are just a few examples of how Jesus will take care of people who are neglected and regarded as ordinary. Because of His kindness, the book of Psalms described Jesus as the Messiah who will be a refuge for the oppressed, with promises that He will bring justice to the poor and powerless and save the children of the needy.

It is therefore needless to overemphasize that the rule of Jesus will be characterized by care and compassion for every human being.

JESUS LOVED PEOPLE AND TAUGHT WHAT IT MEANS TO LOVE

On matters concerning love, Jesus did not only use words, but He also showed through His actions what it means to love. He once said, "If you love those who love you, what credit is that to you? For even sinners love those who love them. And if you do good to those who do good to you, what credit is that to you? For even sinners do the same."

On the other hand, Jesus said, "But love your enemies, do good, and lend, hoping for nothing in return; and your reward will be great, and you will be sons of the Most High. For He is kind to the unthankful and evil. Therefore be merciful, just as your Father also is merciful."[35]

Jesus also said that we must treat others as we would like others to treat us. This is the foundation of the principle commonly referred to as the "golden rule." In his famous Sermon on the Mount, Jesus said:

---

[34]   Matthew 8:2–3.

[35]   Luke 6:32–36.

"Therefore, whatever you want men to do to you, do also to them, for this is the Law and the Prophets."[36] In other words, you are encouraged to love your neighbor and to do good to all, without expecting the same in return.

Jesus used words gently and followed them up with powerful actions that touched the hearts of His listeners to illustrate the true meaning of the love that people should cultivate. He even prayed on behalf of those who were responsible for His death. Jesus prayed for those who crucified Him: "Father, forgive them, for they do not know what they do."[37]

If you consider the way Jesus lived when He was on earth, you will inarguably conclude that His every move was determined by His love to do the will of His Father and His love for mankind. In fact, the Jesus way is the way of love.

Because of this standard set by Jesus on love, the Scriptures gave an accurate interpretation of what love is all about in First Corinthians 13:4–7 (ESV), which says:

> Love is patient and kind; love does not envy or boast; it is not arrogant or rude. It does not insist on its own way; it is not irritable or resentful; it does not rejoice at wrongdoing, but rejoices with the truth. Love bears all things, believes all things, hopes all things, endures all things.

While these words were written in the Bible to show us the meaning of true love, if you look around you—no matter in which part of the

---

[36] Matthew 7:12.
[37] Luke 23:34.

world you live, and especially in the movies—you will find it almost impossible to see this kind of love.

Though this love might seem unattainable in our current system of things, the new theocratic government to be led by Jesus will guarantee that inherent cruelty associated with hatred and warfare will no longer exist. Under His reign, mankind "shall beat their swords into plowshares, and their spears into pruning hooks; nation shall not lift up sword against nation, neither shall they learn war anymore."[38]

On top of this, the Bible promises that peace will flow "like a river," and no longer will families and children suffer the consequences of war, because the coming King will reign in righteousness. And regarding children all over the world, the Bible assures us that no longer will any child be abducted or kidnapped and molested. In contrast to the world of today, where horrible crimes take place even in the most beautiful and supposedly peaceful settings, safety and security will be commonplace. The compassionate rule of Jesus will be like a mother who comforts her own children.

On another level, Jesus is also coming to set prisoners free, and He will free "those who sit in darkness from the prison house"[39] all over the world for crimes they did not commit. Those suffering at the hands of brutal and tyrannical systems of government, and those who are bound spiritually by all sorts of addictions that are beyond their control will be set free as well.

To all peoples in these groups, the Bible assures us that Jesus will declare "liberty to the captives, and the opening of the prison to those

---

[38]   Isaiah 2:4 ESV.
[39]   Isaiah 42:7.

who are bound."[40] Therefore, I would implore you not to give up hope, rather to chin up and hold fast to His promise, which He gave in the Scriptures, in Matthew 11:28–30: Here Jesus says:

> Come to Me, all you who labor and are heavy laden, and I will give you rest. Take My yoke upon you and learn from Me, for I am gentle and lowly in heart, and you will find rest for your souls. For My yoke is easy and My burden is light.

Nevertheless, the largest group of prisoners that Jesus will set free is all of humanity, which has been held captive under the rule of Satan and sin for so long. It is time to rejoice and be full of hope and beautiful expectations, because the new government of Jesus is coming to set the world free. Regardless of their circumstances, everyone will have the opportunity to build a new life in a new system governed by the knowledge and wisdom of God.

WHAT IS JESUS DOING NOW?

In our present system of things, we are used to the selection process and campaigns that happen before any election. This is the way that humans choose their leaders, especially in democratic and sometimes not-so-democratic countries of the world.

During election seasons, the people are bombarded with realistic and unrealistic promises from politicians. Prospective leaders spend huge amounts of money to influence the media in order to get their messages across and convince people to go out and vote for them.

---

[40] Isaiah 61:1.

And after elections, the promises are forgotten, and everyone goes back to square one—to the status quo of broken promises. It goes without saying that we are all used to that.

However, unlike the present system mentioned above that we are used to, the new theocratic government with Jesus as ruler, which will replace all the systems of government in the world today, has already been determined and chosen for us by God.

All we need to do is to decide for ourselves whether to book a spot in this new world. It can be compared to buying a life-insurance policy—only this policy will buy us the assured reality of living forever.

In order to make this chance available for everyone, Jesus is now directing a worldwide campaign of preaching work by His true followers. And He is doing this even as you are reading this book. Many followers of Jesus all over the world are participating in bringing the good news of the kingdom to people. Some are visiting people right now, going from door to door to show them what the Bible says about the coming kingdom of God.

Others are using literature and all kinds of print and digital media to inform people in different regions of the world, in thousands of languages, about what this theocratic government will do for mankind. Even those in prison, as well as those on remote islands, are not left out.

This is a massive worldwide campaign, and it can only be accomplished by divine spiritual direction to make sure that no one is left behind, and this is what Jesus is coordinating. Because of this important campaign effort, Jesus said He would continue to support the work of His disciples until God's kingdom brings an end to human governments.

To confirm His involvement in this ongoing worldwide coverage to bring this information to people all over the world, the Bible says in Matthew 24:14, "And this gospel of the kingdom will be preached in all the world as a witness to all the nations, and then the end will come." Surely, it is only through the involvement of Jesus Christ that this massive project can be accomplished.

Therefore, whether you have heard this good news before or you are hearing it for the first time, I would suggest that you pay attention to understand what it means, because this will be a change of government like no other. It would be wise to be well informed so you can make the best decision for yourself and your little ones who are not mature enough to decide for themselves.

WHAT WILL GOD'S RULERSHIP ACHIEVE FOR MANKIND?

When we listen to the news, we are constantly reminded that the terrible things happening on earth are not what we want and not what God wants either. Jesus witnessed this firsthand when He was on earth. Because of this, He taught us to pray for God's kingdom to come.

But knowing that human beings have the tendency to let things get out of hand before resorting to the fire-brigade approach, our Heavenly Father and our future Ruler did not leave us to keep drifting, hoping to stay afloat long enough to be rescued at the appointed time from this perilous sea.

That is why we must apply insight to note that despite worsening world conditions, Jesus is fully equipped with the knowledge of what it means to be human. He has done many things to help people around the world, and He is continuing to do so. And thanks to the global, Bible-educational preaching work that He foretold in the Scriptures, many are now learning and applying in their daily lives spiritual principles based on Bible knowledge.

He has ensured that millions of people are learning to have a balanced view of their work, as well as improving their family life, in order to enjoy material things without being slaves to them. He is bringing more and more awareness through different learning channels for people to benefit themselves and become the kind of people God wants as citizens of His kingdom.

All the citizens of God's kingdom under the rulership of Jesus will witness the uprooting of the following entrenched pillars of our present system of things. These seemingly unmovable monoliths will be uprooted and removed by Jesus: Namely:

- *False Religion.* All religions that have taught lies about God and have persecuted people and made life difficult for people will be gone forever, and all those who have died at the hands of false religion both in the past and present will be resurrected and given the chance to live their lives to the full as they were meant to be, as explained in First Thessalonians 4:14.

The status of religion as we know it will be done away with forever, because it has caused a lot of problems in the world. The Bible portrays false religion colorfully as a prostitute, and this shameless prostitute will not be allowed to entice and deceive people in the new world.

Sadly, there are many who are benefitting from false religion, and sure enough, they will try to resist this change. Nevertheless, the days of this prostitute are numbered, and her destruction will come as a shock to those who have invested heavily in her lascivious influence, intoxicating power, and arrogance.

- *Human Government.* All over the world, there are prophetic and symbolic signs and very complicated developments reminding us that the tribulations mentioned in the Bible are already upon us and will increase in intensity as time goes on. Meanwhile, in all corners of the globe, everyone will have the opportunity to hear the remarkable message of God's kingdom from the preaching process supported by Jesus. Thus, all mankind will be warned of the forthcoming change that will bring an end to all kinds of human government.

The worldwide preaching work will also serve as a reminder to all the rulers of this world that their impressive high positions will not stop this coming theocratic government, but they can use their high positions to facilitate this important once-in-a-lifetime project. They will be considered and given a chance to choose just like the rest of the people they rule. Therefore, in their peculiar positions as rulers, it would be regarded as good judgement to wise up to what happened to King Nebuchadnezzar, so as not to defy God.

This will surely happen, because human rulership as we know it will not be allowed to exist parallel to God's kingdom. The kingdom of God will put an end to all forms of human government. This must happen to fulfill the Bible prophecy described in Revelation 19:15–16. And it says:

> Out of His mouth goes a sharp sword, that with it He should strike the nations. And He Himself will rule them with a rod of iron. He Himself treads the winepress of the fierceness and wrath of Almighty God. And He has on His robe and on His thigh a name written: KING OF KINGS AND LORD OF LORDS.

- *Wicked People.* The rebuilding of the earth will be a worthwhile and progressive effort that will be a thing of joy to observe, as diverse people of all creeds work together for the common good of all.

However, judging by what we know about humans, it would not be wrong to ask, what about those who are determined to do what is bad and who refuse to obey God? Jesus has this scenario already covered, because the Bible assures mankind in Proverbs 2:22 that "the wicked will be cut off from the earth, and the unfaithful will be uprooted from it." This means that in the new system of things, there will be zero tolerance for bad behavior and wickedness.

- *Satan and His Demons.* The one thing that all humans agree about Satan and his demons is that he is a tireless worker who never sleeps or rests. His legions work nonstop, round the clock, to mislead people and governments into making wrong choices every day.

But his days are also numbered, because very soon he will be neutralized and rendered useless by Jesus. For, just as in previous cases, the Bible has already predicted what will happen to Satan. In the Scriptures, Revelation 20:3 describes what will happen to him. Here, speaking of what Jesus will do, it says:

> And He [Jesus] cast him [Satan] into the bottomless pit, and shut him up, and set a seal on him, so that he should deceive the nations no more till the thousand years were finished. But after these things he must be released for a little while.

And the promise does not end with the demise of Satan. For those who accept God's kingdom, there is much more to expect from Jesus, because He has promised to eliminate the bad and worst conditions and replace them with the good and the very best of any condition imaginable:

- *Sickness and Death Will Be No More.* Everyone will enjoy good health, and sickness and death will be a thing of the past. That is why we are reassured in Isaiah 33:24 (ESV) that "no inhabitant will say, 'I am sick,'" and death will be no more.
- *Jesus Will Ensure True Peace and Security.* Everyone will feel safe, and there will be no need for a police force, armed forces, FBI, CIA, MI6, KGB, FSB, or other spy agency. This is also confirmed in the Scriptures, which reaffirm that "great shall be the peace of your children," and "they shall sit every man under his vine and under his fig tree, and no one shall make them afraid."[41]

---

[41]   Isaiah 54:13; Micah 4:4 ESV.

- *God Will Provide Meaningful Work for Everyone.* There will be enough work to do for everybody—especially in matters concerning the environment—and there will be truly exciting new things to learn and discover.

Regarding the issue of work, the Scriptures say that "My chosen shall long enjoy the work of their hands. They shall not labor in vain."[42] And, with regards to the environment, Isaiah 35:1 says, "The wilderness and the wasteland shall be glad for them, and the desert shall rejoice and blossom as the rose."

Jesus's main objective is that no one is left behind to perish due to lack of knowledge. He wants all people in His kingdom. Therefore, He will teach people not to focus on material things that characterize the old world, but rather to have faith and trust that only God's kingdom will transform the earth to be the way God created it to be in the beginning. He will also provide everyone with the opportunity of helping to rebuild the earth to its original paradise.

To remove every iota of doubt in the minds of people that Jesus will help them to re-establish their broken relationship with God, John 17:3 reassures mankind that "this is eternal life, that they may know You, the only true God, and Jesus Christ whom You have sent."

Furthermore, in order to break it down in a way that everyone will understand, in John 14:6, the apostle reports Jesus's own words—as he was a witness to this fact—where Jesus answered, "I am the way, the truth, and the life. No one comes to the Father except through Me."

---

[42]   Isaiah 65:22–23 ESV.

However, for the sake of those who are not Christians and those of other beliefs who may wonder why Jesus made such an audacious statement, I humbly remind you that the first human being, Adam, was created perfect and without sin, but he chose to disobey God, and because of this, all humans are sinners.

On the other hand, Jesus is perfect. He never sinned; In spite of all the trials He faced while on earth—even when faced with death. So, the death of Jesus proved that a human being could remain loyal to God despite being faced with the most difficult of tests.

Therefore, because Adam died in sin and Jesus died without sin, the Bible in First John 2:2 says concerning Jesus, "He Himself is the propitiation [atoning sacrifice] for our sins, and not for ours only but also for the whole world." In other words, just as Adam's disobedience contaminated the human family with sin, so did the death of Jesus remove the stain of sin from all humans who exercise faith in Him.

This means that because Jesus willingly died on our behalf, He has removed this blemish and repurchased humankind as His own. As a result of this, if anyone does commit sin, we now have a helper who can intercede on our behalf with the Father. In fact, Jesus has cancelled the death sentence for all humans who choose to exercise faith in Him.

Notwithstanding that we still have a limited life span, God has promised, because of what Jesus did, that He will grant righteous humans everlasting life and even go as far as to resurrect those who have died so they can benefit from Jesus's sacrificial death. All of this will be a reality to be witnessed by many who will live in a new world ruled by Jesus as King.

By means of the Bible, God has revealed to humans His master plan to establish a new kingdom that will replace the broken system of the present world as we know it. But the question now for many is--how can humans have the sort of life that God is preparing for those who love and obey Him? And what do they have to do to benefit from this offer to live a glorious life on earth forever?

THE ROAD TO A BETTER LIFE

Millions of people all over the world are looking to find the road to a better life, and they want to know how they can benefit from the promised kingdom of God, but they are disillusioned and disappointed by religions that also are guilty of contributing to the sorry state of things in the world today.

Because of this unenviable reputation, I would say that you may not need to belong to any religious organization or denomination as the only way to enter the kingdom of God. However, you need to know the Bible. This means you must read the Scriptures to help you pick up the pace on your spiritual development.

This is necessary because "all Scripture is given by inspiration of God, and is profitable for doctrine, for reproof, for correction, for instruction in righteousness."[43]

I assume there are many among us who have never read the Bible before, or they have had no former contact with religion, or maybe they don't know where to start, yet they want to find the road that leads to

---

[43]   Second Timothy 3:16.

the kingdom of God. For them I would suggest visiting a Christian gathering or listening to someone preaching the Word of God at least once, to know how to use the Bible as a learning tool and to find spiritual guidance to help them on their way.

Once you get started, I reassure you, you will develop knowledge steadily and will be amazed at how fast your life will begin to change. You will gradually come to know that learning to please the only true God may require making some changes. Never mind that it might seem challenging in the beginning. In the long run, it is a delightful journey like no other, and it begins with you taking the first step to find knowledge.

As you are reading this book, I want to congratulate you for making up your mind to take that first step. I would use this opportunity to inform you of what God has in store for those that seek Him. In First Corinthians 2:9, it says, "But, as it is written: 'What no eye has seen, nor ear heard, nor the heart of man imagined…God has prepared for those who love Him'" (ESV).

It is highly beneficial to use the Bible as a GPS navigator directing you on the road to everlasting life. That is why God said that there is a road you need to take, the road leading off into life, and few are finding it.[44] Further, in Isaiah 48:17, He says, "I am the LORD [Jehovah] your God, who teaches you to profit, who leads you by the way you should go." Therefore, rest assured, walking on this road will lead you to the best life possible.

---

[44]   Matthew 7:14.

The Bible will also help you to understand what Jesus meant when He said, "I am the way, the truth, and the life." Because it is by believing the truths He taught and by imitating the example He set that we can draw close to God and benefit ourselves.

However, there are other requirements everyone must fulfill in order to be members of God's theocratic kingdom: These further instructions are stated below:

REPENT. It is a fact that all have sinned and fallen short of the glory of God. Therefore, the first step on the road to ultimate salvation is genuine and heartfelt repentance. That is why the Apostle Peter wrote in Acts 3:19, "Repent therefore and be converted, that your sins may be blotted out."

Jesus also continually stressed the importance of repentance. He stated, "I have not come to call the righteous, but sinners, to repentance."[45] By declaring this, He plainly means that our highest priority in life should be not to miss out on the kingdom of God. Surely, it would be wise to remember that God responds favorably to a repentant sinner, with total forgiveness made possible by the sacrifice His Son Jesus made to save us.

So, when is the best time to repent?

Now is the right time to repent. Please do not wait, because ominous clouds of global turmoil are gathering on the horizon. Even the Scriptures have already warned us in Acts 17:30, saying, "Truly, these times of ignorance God overlooked, but now commands all men everywhere to repent."

---

[45]   Luke 5:32.

REPENTANCE! WHAT DOES IT MEAN?

Repentance is not some complicated ethereal concept beyond the reach of ordinary people, which no one can fully grasp. In its most basic sense, repentance means to change our minds, change our way of thinking, change our behavior, and change our priorities in order to change our lives.

This change in our lives will be demonstrated in our changed way of living. It is therefore a change from our previous lifestyle that will show the genuineness of our repentance. For instance, Ephesians 4:28 says, "Let him who stole steal no longer, but rather let him labor, working with his hands what is good, that he may have something to give him who has need."

On the flip side, repentance is in no way whatsoever professing to know God but showing no admirable change in their lives, as many preachers in high places do. Rather, it means producing "fruits worthy of repentance," or visible positive changes in our lives that clearly demonstrate that we now indeed put God first in our lives. In fact, repentance produces a humble and submissive heart that seeks and even begs for the mercy of God.

For anyone seeking the kingdom of God, when you reach this stage of your journey you will know that you are ready to take the next fundamental step of asking a true minister of God for baptism for the forgiveness of your sins. Your baptism is a way of identifying yourself with the death and resurrection of Jesus in a public display of faith.

Finally, on repentance and baptism, I would advise you to carefully examine the Scriptures to verify what it says so you can act on what you have learned. With this knowledge, you can now be a beneficiary of that life-insurance policy I mentioned at the beginning of this chapter that God has already provided for all His children, because "it is your Father's good pleasure to give you the kingdom" He promised.[46]

CHOOSE TO SUPPORT GOD'S KINGDOM. The coming of God's kingdom can be compared to a dangerous hurricane heading toward your area, with all the government agencies issuing urgent warnings: "GET OUT! SEEK REFUGE NOW!" Sure enough, the wise thing certainly would be to head for a safe place.

In a sense, comparable to the impending disaster of a hurricane, all of mankind is living in the path of a devastating storm that the Bible refers to as the "Great Tribulation." We cannot simply get out of the path of this tribulation, but we can do something to protect ourselves by seeking first the kingdom of God.

This means that everyone must view God's kingdom as being more important than anything else. To stress the importance of this, Jesus said, "The kingdom of heaven is like a merchant seeking beautiful pearls, who, when he had found one pearl of great price, went and sold all that he had and bought it."[47] In this simple manner, Jesus was trying to illustrate His kingdom so that humans can begin to grasp its vital meaning and significance.

SEEK TO DO GOD'S WILL AND SEEK HIS RIGHTEOUSNESS. We should try our best to live by God's laws and principles as laid out in the Bible, despite the disappointing fact that many churches

---

[46]   Luke 12:32.
[47]   Matthew 13:45–46.

THE KING OF KINGS

and religious organizations have lost their way, sidetracked humanity into believing all kinds of unbiblical philosophies, and propagated a witches' brew of false and misleading gospels.

Even though fake preachers know Jesus warned in Matthew 7:21, "Not everyone who says to Me, 'Lord, Lord,' shall enter the kingdom of heaven, but he who does the will of My Father in heaven," they continue preaching in their misleading ways as if they find joy in tickling their own ears.

On the other hand, the Bible is available for everyone to use as a principled guidebook to live by God's standard, because it is written as a testimony to show that people will certainly enter the kingdom of God, and all true Christians will surely participate and have their part in it.

Having received this assurance based on accurate Bible knowledge, it would be wise to heed the warning of Jesus. He cautioned that some people might get carried away with the shiny objects of this system of things, thinking they can find security in making as much money as possible. And others may let the anxieties of life overwhelm them to the point that they have no attention to seek the life-saving Word of God.

Nevertheless, He promised in Matthew 6:33 that those who support God's kingdom will have what they need now and enjoy endless blessings in the future. Moreover, mankind has already been warned that difficult times will be upon us just before the changeover to God's kingdom.

This warning was not given to make us tremble in fear. Rather, it is written to help us prepare for what is coming so it does not take anyone by surprise. We can use this warning to develop a strong faith to live by the words of Jesus. Knowing ahead that these things must occur before the kingdom comes will help us to face even the severest of problems. And sure enough, we are not left alone, for through faith, God gives us power beyond what is normal to cope with things that might appear to be beyond our capability. This is the real power that God gives those who have faith in Him, as described in Second Corinthians 4:18: "We do not look at the things which are seen, but at the things which are not seen. For the things which are seen are temporary, but the things which are not seen are eternal."

So, how can we respond to the good news?

The Bible encourages us to accept the message with the greatest eagerness of mind, to carefully examine the Scriptures to verify what we have heard, and to act on what we have learned.

TELL OTHERS ABOUT THE KINGDOM OF GOD. It is encouraging to learn that around the world, millions of people have taken steps to support God's kingdom. You can do the same by telling your family members and your friends about what you have learned. You can help them to carefully examine the Scriptures, and you can show them that you want to serve Him and above all that God wants everyone to serve Him.

Finally, help them to understand that what you are doing is not extraordinary. It is written in the Scriptures, in Matthew 24:14, that "this gospel [good news] of the kingdom will be preached in all the world as a witness to all the nations, and then the end will come."

WHEN WILL GOD'S KINGDOM RULE THE EARTH?

From what is written in the Bible, it is correct to say that God's kingdom will come as soon as the worldwide preaching work of the good news is complete. This means that everyone alive must hear about the coming of the kingdom of God as a witness to them and thereby be given the opportunity to either choose God's kingdom or stand against it.

Meanwhile, even as the world is experiencing dreadful problems, several millions of people from all nations are declaring and preaching the good news of God's kingdom in many lands and in thousands of languages, and some of them are doing this in very difficult conditions.

If you take a moment to consider this information, you will realize how awesome this is, because this has never happened before in human history. However, there are events that Jesus Christ foretold, and these events are happening today—even as you are reading this book.

When Jesus was on earth, some of His faithful followers wanted to know when God's kingdom would begin to rule the earth. He answered their question by saying that they would not know exactly when that would occur. However, He cautioned that when they saw a certain group of events happening all at once, they would know that the kingdom of God was near and the time for it to rule the world had come.

It is remarkable to learn that Jesus gave this answer to His followers some two thousand years ago. This shows that even back then, men knew that mankind was headed in the wrong direction. Fast-forward to the year 2022, and people around the world are wondering if the end of the world is near.

If you would pause for a moment to think about it, you will realize that there has never been such a widespread interest in this topic as there is today. And who can blame people for wondering, when you yourself are a living witness to what is happening to our world.

I would say that the signs of the end are prevalent all over the world, and the evidence is very clear—to the extent that anyone willing to accept the truth can see. The end is creeping closer and closer, to conclude this unsustainable way of living. However, it would be wise to consider the events foretold by Jesus in the Bible and use them as a guideline to obtain accurate understanding. So, what events did Jesus say would happen? In Luke 21:10–11, He said to His followers: "Nation will rise against nation, and kingdom against kingdom. And there will be great earthquakes in various places, and famines and pestilences; and there will be fearful sights and great signs from heaven."

Some of these occurrences are already happening at a rapid tempo all over the world.

For Example:

*WARS

If we are to consider the evidence that nation will rise against nation and kingdom against kingdom, it is clear Jesus was talking about wars. Nonetheless, it is also correct to say that there have always been wars at every stage of human history, and it is in the nature of humans to fight amongst themselves.

But this human flaw notwithstanding, in 1914, war broke out on a scale never seen before in all of human history. It marked the beginning of the first-ever World War. The war introduced the first large-scale use of tanks, aerial bombs, machine guns, and poisonous gas. Not long after, it was followed by the second World War, and this war introduced the design, manufacture, and use of atomic weapons by humans against other humans.

Sadly enough, mankind has been fighting wars in one place or another ever since, and even as you are reading this book, there's a war going on somewhere on earth, and all these wars have killed millions of people.

*EARTHQUAKES

According to *Britannica Academic,* there are about one hundred earthquakes that are large enough to cause substantial damage every year. With trepidation, in the last ten years, we have witnessed a dramatic rise in both the frequency and intensity of these earthquakes. It might be regarded as just a coincidence, but rarely a month goes by without a strong earthquake occurring somewhere in the world.

Whichever way we view it, the fact is that earthquakes and tsunamis that occur in the sea around the world are causing suffering and loss of life on an unprecedented scale, and it is happening more frequently than ever before.

*FAMINES AND FOOD SHORTAGES

In human history, there has never been more money and financial wealth in the world as there is right now in our present time. Yet, the World Food Programme reported in 2022: "As many as 828 million people go to bed hungry every night, the number of those facing acute food insecurity has soared—from 135 million to 345 million—since 2019."[48]

It would be correct to point out that this is partly caused by famines and unproductive land from global warming and natural disasters. Despite these factors, food shortages occur worldwide mainly because of war, corruption, economic collapse, poor management of agriculture, and general lack of vision by those in leadership positions.

These man-made factors and irresponsible behavior of human leaders have contributed to the death of about 3.1 million children who die from malnutrition every year. It is sad to note that this alone was the cause of about 45 percent of all child deaths worldwide, and yet, all these were foretold in the Bible before our present time.

*PESTILENCES

It is not an exaggeration to state that most of us have just lived through a few years that are unprecedented in human history. Many people alive today have no memory of a time in the past when pandemic brought the world almost to a standstill or shut down entire economies. Some would have thought you were crazy if you had told them that in 2020 that their way of life would include a few kilometers' travel to the supermarket and a curfew that would limit their movement to only within their city limits.

Yet, the twenty-first century had already been marked by major epidemics. The World Health Organization warned in its publication

---

[48]   "A Global Food Crisis," World Food Programme, 2022, wfp.org/global-hunger-crisis.

that old diseases like cholera, plague, and yellow fever have reemerged, and new ones like Ebola, SARS, MERS, and, most recently, COVID-19 have emerged.

Even though scientists, virologists, and medical doctors have learned much about sicknesses in the past fifty years, they have not been able to find a cure for all diseases. However, with the coronavirus disrupting life as we know it and causing global panic—which you have the right to interpret any way you want—pandemics are simply a reminder that we are living in a dying world.

But these are not the only signs foretold in the Bible, because—in as much as these things mentioned above are happening in the world—there are other signs concerning the attitude of humans in the last days to be considered as well. For example, Second Timothy 3:1–5 says regarding the last days:

> But know this, that in the last days perilous times will come: For men will be lovers of themselves, lovers of money, boasters, proud, blasphemers, disobedient to parents, unthankful, unholy, unloving, unforgiving, slanderers, without self-control, brutal, despisers of good, traitors, headstrong, haughty, lovers of pleasure rather than lovers of God, having a form of godliness but denying its power.

Finally, it concludes, "And from such people turn away!" As you can see for yourself, you don't have to look far to see that these verses predict the great moral degeneration in human societies today.

I know that some diehard defenders of this system of things will argue that there is nothing surprising about all of this because it is the nature of mankind, and the world has always been this way. Nevertheless, whether this argument is true or false, it would be wise to seek knowledge from the Bible to confirm if these patterns point to the last days.

For example, on issues concerning:

*TERRIBLE TIMES

Are we living in terrible times? Of course! It is obvious we are living in perilous times. For instance, many people are disenchanted with the leadership of their respective countries, both in democratic and undemocratic nations. There are uprisings all over the world, with people protesting and rioting and sometimes with serious consequences of general instability and government overthrow.

People are becoming increasingly aware of the power they have if they band together. They are risking bodily harm, death, imprisonment, and exile in order to force a change from their leaders who have remained obstinate to their demands for a better life. Their powerless agitation to sway their leaders has manifested in many documented cases of terrorism, economic turmoil, and political revolutions, with violence at the tipping point of their frustrations.

*PEOPLE WILL BE LOVERS OF THEMSELVES

Mankind is now living in a covetous age in a world where people clamor after the latest things—a world that is solely focused on "what's in it for me." Love thy neighbor as thyself has turned into a cliché that has little or no meaning in the mouths of many but has been replaced with a selfish, self-focused, and self-consuming view of "me" before others.

This phenomenon is widespread and can be observed in every corner of the globe. Sadly, this fast-growing narcissism in human societies reflects the absence of true love as exemplified by the love of Christ for humans. It is a regrettable sign of the times that many have forgotten how beautiful a day can be when love and kindness touch it.

*CHILDREN WILL BE DISOBEDIENT TO THEIR PARENTS

In the world of today, there is a steady and significant increase of lawlessness among youths, and there is evidence that many youths are revolting against parental authority. For instance, in the last decade alone, in the three great economies of the United States, China, and the United Kingdom, it is reported that juvenile arrests for violent crimes have increased more than 200 percent, and the overall rate of juvenile arrests for other crimes is growing at more than 10 percent a year. This is twice the adult rate in the same period. Also, in many countries around the world, there are constant reports of juveniles involved in murder, fraud, theft, rape, drug trafficking, and gang banging.

Other reports show a steady pattern of brazen violence directed toward parents. Many sociologists around the globe are confronted with a disturbing trend that shows that more than two and a half million adolescents have admitted to having struck their parent at least once. And a majority of the parents of these adolescents were either punched, bit, kicked, beat up, threatened with a knife, or had a gun used on them.

Many young people are engaging in sexual promiscuity as a way to go against their parents' wishes, and some teenagers use alcoholic drinks and addictive drugs to express their disobedience. Many social workers who are in regular contact with many youths have also concluded that smoking marijuana is a regular pastime of many teenagers, and many deliberately disobey by refusing to be persuaded to follow their parents' moral or religious standards.

To make matters worse, many youths spend most of their time watching television and playing video games laced with low moral content. Most of their behaviors are copied from films and television, which is constantly bombarding their minds with reckless violence and immorality.

However, parents should never give up on their children, just as our Heavenly Father never gave up on us. Moreover, the Scriptures make it clear to every parent that "he who spares his rod hates his son, but he who loves him disciplines him promptly."[49]

On this note, the Bible instructs every father in Ephesians 6:4: "Fathers, do not provoke your children to wrath, but bring them up in the training and admonition of the Lord." This means that even though we are living in the last days, it is wrong for a parent to succumb to permissive child-rearing social theories prevalent in our societies today, because this will result in raising a child that is a tyrant or sure to be one when he or she becomes an adult.

*MANY PEOPLE WILL BE UNHOLY

Referring to this sign of the last days, it would be wise to note that the Bible has already confirmed that all of mankind has sinned and

---

[49]   Proverbs 13:24.

come short of the glory of God. Nevertheless, this unholy attitude of mankind should be particularly concerning to those professing to be Christians, who have the advantage of the knowledge of the teachings of Jesus Christ.

If you were to compare the attitude of many Christians today to the behavior of many Christians several decades ago, you will notice that many were humble and morally sound in their lifestyle in past days, as compared to how people are today. Instead, we have a lot of Christians who believe it is no longer necessary to keep godly commandments so long as they believe in Jesus Christ. Yet, their behavior calls into question their belief in Jesus.

Many of these modern-day Christians can be found in churches and houses of worship all over the globe, and because of this attitude, houses that have been dedicated to the worship of the only true God are now full of unconverted, unholy people and false preachers who have turned their religious knowledge into a license to sin. It is embarrassing to say that many churches have adopted the funky style of jamboree events, with more resemblance to theaters and concert halls than holy places of worship.

With this new image of Christianity, many non-Christians are left in a no-man's-land to wander in search of true Christianity, while professing Christians seem to think that they will be saved in their sins because of their pretense, rather than being saved through repentance, forgiveness, and doing the will of God.

Regarding this global religious confusion, the Scriptures foretold in Second Timothy 4:3–4, "The time will come when...they will turn their ears away from the truth, and be turned aside to fables." And the book of Revelation refers to false religious systems as "Babylon," which is another word for "confusion," where it says, "Babylon is fallen, is fallen, that great city, because she has made all nations drink of the wine of the wrath of her fornication."[50]

This wine is the worldwide teaching of false gospels that lead many away from the true teachings of Jesus Christ.

This particular sign shows that there is very little effort made today to turn away from sin and to live a life according to the example shown by Jesus Christ, even among Christians. So, if people who have the knowledge of the Bible are so casual about their personal lifestyle, then what will be the attitude of those who do not have this knowledge? Your guess is as good as mine.

*THERE WILL BE AN INCREASE IN KNOWLEDGE

More than at any period in human history, there is a visible increase in knowledge beyond previous generations. This increase in knowledge shows that toward the end of this system of things, a majority of humans will have the opportunity unavailable to former generations to read and acquire general knowledge in almost any subject and to understand the Word of God.

During this period leading up to the end, millions of people who are seeking knowledge in every aspect of life, including the knowledge of God, will have a vast array of choices from which to obtain wisdom.

---

[50]   Revelation 14:8.

And many will have the tools to learn the Word of God to help them prepare for the end.

For instance, in recent years, the world has gone increasingly digital. This means anyone can use modern technology to source and obtain information through their personal computers, tablets, and mobile phones. You can even download You Version into your mobile phone. This Bible app for mobile devices has over a hundred million downloads, and it gives the user the opportunity to have information from the Bible at his or her fingertips.

There is also the Bible Hub app, which many prefer because it gives the user instant access to many translations and definitions and provides simplified Bible commentaries on various topics and devotions.

It is on record that more than 66,000 people are using a Bible app worldwide at any given minute, and because of this, more than 77 percent of people say they are reading the Bible more frequently because they have it available on their mobile devices.

It is remarkable that during the dark periods of human history, there were only a few copies of the Bible anywhere on earth, and these copies were among the priceless possessions of kings and rulers. And even more remarkable is the fact that men gave their lives in order to make the Bible available to ordinary people.

However, since then, copies of the Bible have slowly and surely multiplied, and the printing and translating of the Bible into different languages has also increased. It is therefore a joy to report that since the printing of the first copy, the Bible is by far the most widely translated, distributed, and purchased book in all of human history to date.

Over a hundred million Bibles are printed every year in more than 2,100 languages, and all over the world there are more than eighty thousand different versions of the Bible available for people to choose from. The annual sales of all versions of the Bible sold worldwide routinely top $400 million, and the estimated total sales of Bibles have now exceeded six billion copies.

So, what happened, and why is the Bible so popular?

For most of human history, very few people had access to the Bible, many were not privileged to own it, and some people were killed because they wanted to make it possible for everyone to read the Bible.

The Bible is very popular because God wants everyone to know about Him and learn the truth about His will for humans. This means that God is using the Bible to ensure that many have the opportunity to gain accurate knowledge, as foretold in Daniel 12:4. Regarding increasing knowledge, the prophetic book of Daniel declares:

> But you, Daniel, shut up the words, and seal the book until the time of the end; many shall run to and fro, and knowledge shall increase.

Based on this prophecy, one can gain understanding as to what times the Bible is referring to and what time we are living in right now in the world. All you need to do is look at the tremendous advancements in information technology and the amazing ability to use computer intelligence to accomplish much more than previous generations.

Accordingly, mankind is not only advancing rapidly in scientific knowledge and technology. We are also gaining spiritual knowledge to help us to understand how God will accomplish his plan in order to benefit the kingdom He has promised us, which will replace the system of things in the world today.

Certainly, due to the widespread use of the Bible all over the world now, more than at any time in history, people are enabled to obtain spiritual knowledge and the wisdom to understand the deep things of God.

Confirming the outpouring of knowledge during this period, the book of Habakkuk referred to spiritual knowledge that will be revealed in the period leading to the last days. Habakkuk 2:14 says:

> For the earth will be filled with the knowledge of the glory of the LORD, as the waters cover the sea.

Finally, we can rest assured that God has rapidly increased the knowledge in the world through various means so that mankind can use it to benefit themselves and gain accurate knowledge concerning His will.

Please help yourself to God's message of salvation coming to you through the television, Internet, satellite networks, and numerous print and digital media, which will surely cover the entire inhabited earth as a witness to all nations.

PART THREE

CONVERSATIONS WITH MY FATHER

There is a voice speaking in the sweet breeze of daylight. Sometimes you can hear it from the top of the mountains or through the crashing waves of the sea, but most of the time it is speaking in the quiet moments of life when you are sleeping or when you are alone.

This is the voice of God. *I am convinced God is talking to us all the time, and only those who listen carefully will hear Him.*

CHAPTER NINE

START BY LISTENING

I cannot fully recall what my first discussion with my Heavenly Father was or what led to this communication because I have not always been a good listener. Looking back now, I am sure that someone was trying to get my attention by means of three important dreams during that period of my youth.

I was ten years old when I first dreamed that I was playing football with my friends in the valley on the outskirts of our village. And there was a hill on the outer edges of our playing field that separates our village from the next.

On this day, I dreamed that we were playing football. I kicked the ball high, and it landed on this hill. So, we decided to climb the hill to retrieve our ball, but no matter how much we tried, none of us could get to the actual spot on the top of the hill where the ball had landed.

We tried and tried, but we could not reach the ball. Suddenly, the sun began to go down, and one by one, all my friends left and went home as darkness was approaching very fast. Yet, I did not want to go back without the ball because I was the one who had kicked it to the top of this hill. So, I continued climbing, and somehow, I got to the spot, picked up the ball, and realized I was standing at the very top of the hill.

When I looked down on the valley on the other side of the hill, I could see there was still daylight. Other kids that looked to be the same age as me were playing football at the bottom of the hill. Some of them looked up and saw me and waved at me to come and join them. I noticed they all looked different from me, because their hair was bright, and their complexion was fair. But when I took a step to go downward to join them, I woke up and realized I had been dreaming.

I could not go back to sleep, so I stayed awake the rest of the night trying to figure out why I could not fall asleep because of a simple dream. But this dream did not leave me alone, because two weeks later, I had this exact same dream, and in the same manner, I could not fall asleep afterward.

The following day, I told my father about my dream. At first, he did not say anything, but when I informed him that I'd had this same dream two times, he paused from what he was doing, looked at me, and said, "I think someone is trying to send you a message." Then he told me he did not know the meaning of this dream. Nonetheless, he said to me, "If you want to know the meaning, you can pray to God to reveal the meaning to you."

I was not satisfied with his answer, so I left it at that. A short period later, I was just about to go out to play with my friends after school when I ran into my father again, and he asked me if I had prayed to God like he'd advised me to do. I told him I did not know how to pray, and praying was only for adults. I said this because as long as I could remember, he was the only one that conducted prayer in our family.

That evening after dinner, my father taught me how to pray. At first, he taught me the Lord's Prayer. He told me to add anything I wanted to ask of or know from God following that prayer. Further, he told me that prayer is very important because it is the best way to communicate with God.

As time went on, because of this occurrence, I noticed that my father began to pay more attention to me, and gradually we developed a close relationship. He would use every opportunity to get me to listen to his Bible readings even though it was obvious I had no interest in such things.

But how can you get a ten-year-old boy to listen? Especially an extrovert like me. I had so much going on in my head that listening was not my favorite activity. Yet, my father understood this, and he tried very much to make me understand the importance of listening.

He must have told me a hundred times to listen. One day, he told me that listening is not just about listening to others, but it also involves listening to oneself.

He said to me, "You may think you know what you are doing, but do you know what is happening to you? Because what is happening to you could be a result of what you are doing. Therefore, if you listen and pay attention to yourself, perhaps you can use what is happening to you to make things better for yourself and for others."

He concluded this discussion between us by reminding me, "Twenty boys do not play for twenty years." I guess that was his way of telling me that time waits for no one.

If I had paid serious attention to his words, I would have realized that he was trying to use simple words to teach me even at that young age the simple basics of the "Law of Rhythm." In order words, he was telling me that I am not going to feel good all the time, that sometimes I will feel low and unhappy, and at other times, I will feel very happy and worthy. Nonetheless, I should use the good feelings of happiness and worthiness to know when I am on the right track.

Ruefully, it was many years before I realized he wanted me to understand the basic principles of cause and effect. He was trying to teach me to listen to my intuition and allow it to guide me to make the right choices.

It felt like a home run when I recalled that he had told me specifically, "Listening to yourself can be compared to 'Man, know thyself,' which simply means you cannot be good in everything or certain things, but there is something you can do better than everyone else, and if you understand this, you can use it to lift up yourself and others as well."

To this day, I still remember his words and how patient he was with me without getting annoyed at my reluctance to embrace his utmost belief in God. And yet his words stuck with me even up until this very day.

But time does not wait for anyone, because in just a few years, I turned twelve and was admitted to a nearby high school. My high school period was mostly filled with schoolwork and football—especially football, as I was selected to play for my school, and from there, I went on to play for my local district juniors.

My coach and many people who saw me play told me I was good and that I had the talent to make it as a professional football player. So, I spent most of my free time in training and on the field with the hope that one day a big club would notice me and help me to fulfill my dream of being a professional footballer. But little did I know then that my way of life would be forced by unforeseen circumstances to take a different direction from what I had envisioned.

During the long holiday at the end of the school year I was called up to play with a selection of our local government district juniors against another district. In this game, I was involved in a serious tackle with another player from the opposing side, and I fractured the ankle on my right leg. I was taken to the hospital in a nearby town, where I was operated on to fix my broken leg.

The operation was successful, but afterward the doctor said to me, "If you want to walk for the rest of your life, I suggest you stop playing football." I did not believe him. I thought he was talking gibberish. There was nothing anyone could have said to me then to change my mind about football. Nevertheless, I spent a very painful six months at home recuperating and learning how to walk normally again. This was the first difficult experience of my young teenage life.

It happened that in this period, my cousin started dating a sailor. One day, this sailor came to visit us, and he told a most unusual story of how he had discovered a young man hiding in the anchor room of their ship on a voyage to Europe. He described how he had found the boy shivering from cold and called the ship's medical officer, who informed the captain, and how they took care of him and handed him over to the authorities when they arrived at the first port on their route.

I was so struck by the courage of the young man to risk his life as a stowaway in order to travel to a faraway land that in the months that followed, this story continued to fascinate me—to the extent that I wondered if I could take a risk like that.

Nonetheless, I had my football—or so I thought—and it was my utmost desire to get back on the field. But during my first game after the operation, I noticed that I could no longer run fast with the ball like I used to, and I was fearful of going into tackles with other players.

Our coach noticed this hesitancy on my part, and he took me off and replaced me with a sub. After the game, he told me he observed that I was afraid and advised me to take time off to consider if there were other things I would like to do—because it is not possible to play football without getting into tackles with other players.

A few months before my sixteenth birthday, war broke out between the northern region of our country and the southern region. The two sides had long been engaged in a political powerplay of ideology, power sharing, and national identity, with the toxic mix of Islam, Christianity, and corruption in the middle. So, it was not really a surprise when the southern states decided to secede from the union of the national government, and because of this the center could no longer hold. The two sides declared war on each other.

I was born in the south, and due to the resulting destruction, deaths, insecurity, and rampant scarcity of food, we were forced to flee our region, thereby interrupting and leaving unfinished an important developmental phase of my life. I felt betrayed by all the adults and the so-called leaders for having robbed my generation of the future we deserved, and because of this, I was bitter and angry for long periods of my young-adult life.

I remembered the story told by the sailor who was dating my cousin, and because of the massive mobilization for young men to fight I headed towards the direction of the nearest seaport that I could find. After several days of hardship, dodging soldiers and war machinery, I arrived at the port. On the night of the second day, I took advantage of the chaos and confusion around the place and climbed into the first less-secured ship I could find via the cable that tied the ship to the dock.

I followed the direction of the anchor chain and traced my way into the chamber, where the cable was rolled into a huge round ball. I was afraid all the time that someone was going to find me and raise the alarm, but since no one did, I decided to stay there as long as possible. All I had to do was to be careful not to get entangled in that heavy chain. And in that place was a small faucet with running water. Moreover, it was also possible to do my toilets in that place and throw it out through the hole and into the water.

I was very tired, and I fell asleep. And in that very place, I had the same dream that I had dreamed years before. Instantly, I was wide awake and realized that the ship was swaying from side to side. There was a gentle breeze coming in through the hole, and I became aware that the ship was slowly sailing out of the harbor.

It was very dark in that chamber, and I was almost about to panic when suddenly it occurred to me that this was the third time, I'd had the same dream. In that moment, it dawned on me that this was the meaning of the dream: I was going to leave my family, my friends, and everything behind to go to a faraway place that I had never heard of before.

In the daytime, it was not so spooky inside there compared to the nighttime, as there was some light coming in through the hole. After looking around, I found an old, discarded sailor's jacket, two buckets of grease, hand gloves, and a tarpaulin, which I used to cover myself in the night.

I did not know where the vessel was heading, and there was no way of telling the time or even the day of the week or date of the month, so I concentrated on staying alive by rationing the bread, the cassava, biscuits, and old newspapers I had brought with me into the ship.

As I got used to the rolling movement of the ship, I began to count the days and I had water and protection from the cold. So, if no one found me, I planned to hide there until I noticed that the ship was no longer moving, and only then was I going to find my way out of that hole.

The days were very long inside there, and I had all the time in the world to think about my parents, my friends, my football coach, my school, my village, and the war I had left behind me. I wondered if I would ever see them again. I made a promise to myself that if I should somehow make it safely out of this boat, I would devote my time to improving myself and seek to know God just like my father wanted me to do.

Meanwhile, it seemed like several weeks have passed since I had climbed onto the ship. Nevertheless, one morning I was awakened by the grinding sound of the anchor cable. I moved back as far as possible from it when I noticed it was gradually unwinding out of the hole and heading into the water. It was then I realized that the ship was no longer rolling from side to side. It had finally come to a stop.

But when I tried to climb out through the hole, the cables started pulling back into the chamber, and in my confusion, I began to panic and lost my courage.

I spent the whole of that day listening to every sound on the decks above, and I decided I was going to leave the ship in the middle of the night when no one was up and about. In the evening of that day, it started to rain, with flashes of lightning and thunder. Somehow, I took this to be a good sign, because all the sailors would be inside their cabins.

It was raining heavily when I made my move. There was no sign of movement above me when I opened the door leading into the hole and made my way to the gangplank linking the ship with the dock. To my surprise, no one stopped me, and even if they observed me, I am sure I must have looked like a seaman in the heavy sailor's jacket.

After I left the ship, I kept walking in the general direction of where I guessed the highway was because of the intermittent flashes of vehicle light that lit that direction. It was my hope that it would lead me out of the seaport. My sole intention was to walk as far as possible and away from that ship. And even in that pouring rain and windy condition, I knew I was no longer in Africa.

I must have walked the whole night in a confused state of mind because I was walking along the motorway when a minivan pulled up beside me. Behind the wheel was a woman in some sort of cleaning uniform who was screaming at me, telling me to get off the road. I guess she must have noticed how miserable I looked or somehow felt sorry for me, because she opened the passenger door of her van and beckoned me to step inside.

I was surprised when she asked me in English, "Are you okay?" I told her yes, I was okay, but that I had been walking the whole night after climbing out of the ship that had brought me to this place. She asked me where I came from, and I told her. It was then she told me that I was in Rotterdam.

Even till this day I will never understand why I started crying and telling her how I had hidden in a ship as a stowaway and about my journey at sea. When she found out how young I was, I noticed that the look on her face changed, and she looked kinder than the first impression I had of her.

After driving for a while, she stopped at the first petrol station along the way and asked me if I was hungry. I said yes, and she went into the station and came back with some snacks and a bottle of Coca-Cola that she gave to me. She then told me that I was lucky she had found me because if I had continued walking along the road, I would have been hit by a car, as it got very busy in the mornings. Or someone would have called the police on me.

She then told me she knew of a place where they take care of people running away from trouble, and she would help me to get there. After that, she wrote an address on a piece of paper and gave it to me, and she drove me to the train station and bought a ticket for me to the city where they have facilities to take care of asylum seekers. She stayed with me to make sure I boarded the right train and even walked me to the train conductor and told him to make sure that I did not miss my stop point.

I will never forget the kindness of that lady, and my only regret is that I never had the courage to ask her name or address. Sometimes,

I wonder what would have happened to me if she had not stopped to pick me up. Even up till this day, I keep hoping that our paths will cross again so I can reward her for the kindness she showed to a stranger who looked totally different from her.

When I look back on my journey so far, I am convinced that the dream I had several years ago was just a tiny peek into the future by the Creator of the universe, to show me His plans for me and how my life would pan out if I put my trust in Him.

True to the words of the lady who helped me on that first day, I received tremendous help from the authorities to the extent that within a few years, I had learned their language and was able to integrate into their society. Although I arrived here without a high school diploma, I was able to graduate from a technical college with a diploma in Transport and Logistics.

Despite the help I have received from strangers and all the efforts I have made to improve myself; I still find it difficult to forget the circumstances that led me to leave my homeland. Because of this, I harbor a strong disdain for politicians and leaders—and I mean all kinds of leaders.

Because of this strong feeling of distrust toward people in power, I began to observe closely the patterns of government in different areas of the world, especially in Europe. I was surprised to see that even in a society such as this, there were people struggling from all kinds of addiction and poverty—many living on the streets with no place to call their own.

I have also come to realize that for reasons I cannot explain, I find it difficult to be in one place for long periods of time, and because of this I decided to become a truck driver so as not to have an affinity to any particular culture but instead to give myself time to determine the best way to live my life.

Due to the nature of my job as a truck driver, I have traveled extensively within the countries of Western Europe and Canada. I have been a long-distance commercial truck driver for the past twenty years, and during this period, I have observed and compared many forms of human rulership, from democracy to socialism to autocracy, communism, and dictatorships.

From my observation, I have realized that they all have one thing in common, and I have noticed that no matter the system in place anywhere, *all the governments have let most of their people down most of the time.*

Based on my discussions during my travels with people from all walks of life, backgrounds, colors, creeds, beliefs, and religions, I am compelled to say that the majority of the people are disappointed with their governments. They feel let down by the worsening conditions of living, inequality, insecurity, non-transparency, lies and manipulation, and corruption playing out in front of their very own eyes every day.

Because of this, I am inclined to conclude that this trend of bad rulership by leaders is not confined to any particular culture, society, or region. Neither is it characteristic of any single human demographic or ethnicity, even though it appears to be more obvious and recognizable in some regions of the world. It is now easy to see that in every region of the world; this trend is manifesting with the same effect on the people according to the entrenched system of rulership in any particular area.

This means that if you live in developing regions of the world, you must not assume that people in developed regions are enjoying fulfillment of their expectations of life, with no worries. Rather, you should be aware that all of creation and all human societies are groaning under the burden of human misrule according to the overwhelming factors on the ground. One of these factors can be just as bad as another, and they are continuously exacerbated and exploited by leaders.

Having arrived at this conclusion, I realized that rather than being angry that I was forced to leave my country, I must devote more time to seeking answers to why our human rulers have turned out to be mostly disappointing so far.

In my search for answers, I have read many books on the different systems of government and found out that although it may seem as if some system of government is theoretically better than others, the problem lies with the interpretation of the theory. Any system can benefit people if leaders are genuinely and selflessly committed to the betterment of their people.

This means that any system can work if the leaders stay focused on making the lives of their people better rather than lording it over their subjects through political power play and self-aggrandizement. To my amazement, I realized that both in democratic and undemocratic countries, majority of the citizens are struggling to make ends meet, as many are slowly working themselves to death just to keep their heads above water. On the other hand, the leaders are living fabulously on the taxes paid by working people and on the perks and privileges usurped from their political portfolio.

All the same, studying the systems of government could not provide a reasonable explanation to satisfy my curiosity, because the foundation of the different systems of government was laid on ambiguity and injustice that have never really been addressed.

In the meantime, while I was still searching, I started reading self-improvement and self-development books. I must admit that I have benefited tremendously from these books because of the guidance from them that I have applied to achieve satisfactory improvements in many areas of my life.

Finally, I thought the churches had the answer on how to make men better leaders for their people. Even though I regard myself as a Christian, I have never really belonged to any Christian denomination. So, I started going to church every Sunday. I must have attended the meetings of more than fifty churches in the southern provinces of the Netherlands before I found out that all the churches were preaching the Gospel in their own style and interpreting the Bible in their own way--telling people to change their ways. Yet, they seemed more interested in increasing membership than in meeting the real needs of individuals to make changes in their lives.

I was not really surprised to find out that all over Europe, most of the leaders call themselves Christians—as well as the majority of the people. But if they are Christians, why do they fall into this trap of bad governance just like leaders in non-Christian nations? I do understand that leaders are not responsible for the wrong decisions that people make, but many citizens suffer for the wrong decisions made at the very top. In fact, many people make wrong decisions due to helplessness and hopelessness, as they feel abandoned by their leaders.

MY PERSONAL EXPERIENCE WITH PRAYER

During my period of searching and trying to make sense of it all, I remembered the advice my father gave to me many years ago. He wanted me to know how to pray and how to use the Bible to gain insight into the will of God for me and to apply it in solving any problem that might come my way. So, for the first time in years, I picked up my Bible and started reading from the first chapter of Genesis.

At first, I was reading out of curiosity, but after a while, I realized that I liked the stories about creation and the origins of mankind. Because of this, I made it a habit to read a few chapters of the Bible every day. During this period, I was most of the time preoccupied in my mind with thinking about the things I was learning from the Bible, and because of this, I would take my Bible with me on all my travels.

Despite my new habit of keeping the Bible close to me, it never occurred to me to pray until one evening after reading. I could no longer reconcile what I was reading with the realities of life I had to face daily. At that time, I was just reading the Bible as any other storybook, with the intention of reading it from cover to cover.

As a truck driver, I only have time to read one or two chapters before retiring for the night, no matter where I stop. But this night was different because after reading, I could not sleep even though I was very tired. So, I prayed to God to help me to understand what I was reading, or else I was going to stop reading the Bible. And I asked Him to help me fall asleep.

I guess I must have fallen asleep instantly, because the following morning I was fit and fresh and ready to go and could not even remember what had happened the previous night. After that night, it seemed as if a new horizon had just opened up for me. From then onwards, I began to pray regularly, and I would never let a day go by without praying to thank God for what I was learning and for His protection.

In the beginning, I was mostly praying for protection because I was driving long distances every day, and I have witnessed many accidents along my way. But one day, I finished loading my truck late in the afternoon in a town in the south of Belgium called La Louviere, on the E42 Motorway in the direction of Charleroi.

While giving me the transport documents for the goods in my trailer, the shipping clerk told me to make sure to be at the delivery address in the city of Strasbourg in the northeast of France before twelve noon the following day.

Because of this extra requirement, I only had a short time limit remaining to find a safe place to park for the evening. I intended to start very early the next morning, and eventually I found a place along the highway close to the towns of Rhisnes and La Bruyère.

However, on this very night I had a terrible dream. I dreamed that I had an accident. My truck slid out of control, and I was trapped in the cabin, hanging precariously downwards into a very steep ravine. This dream was so real, and because it felt like a nightmare, I was instantly awake. But when I realized it was just a bad dream, I prayed and went back to sleep.

Very early the next morning, I drove out of the parking lot, heading in the direction of the city of Liège, when suddenly and out of nowhere, I saw two little puppy dogs running on the highway. It looked like one was chasing the other, and before I could react, the two dogs disappeared under my vehicle. I stepped on my brakes, but it was too late. I must have driven about eighty meters before I managed to stop the vehicle on the shoulder of the highway.

I switched on my hazard lights, picked up my flashlight, and stepped out of the truck. When I stepped onto the tarmac, I noticed there were no headlights behind me and so in the interval I was convinced I was the only one on that stretch of the highway at that time.

I switched on the flashlight and looked thoroughly everywhere under the truck and trailer, but I could not see any blood or sign that I had driven over any animal. So, I continued looking for the dogs, but there were no marks on the road surface. I walked almost a hundred meters behind looking for the dogs, all the time apprehensive that I was going to discover I had killed the two puppies.

I must have been searching for those dogs for a while—maybe twenty minutes—before I saw headlights in the far distance behind me. I looked around me on that part of the highway and noticed that it was a wooded area with trees and bushes on both sides of the road, so I began to wonder to myself, where did those two dogs come from? And where were their dead bodies? What were they doing on the road at that time, because there were no houses and no sign of human activity on that section of the highway. I could only assume that maybe they were blinded by the headlights of my truck. Even so, it never made any sort of sense to me.

After searching in vain without finding anything, I went back to my truck and continued on my journey, but the fear on the faces of those dogs continued to play over and over in my mind—and even till this day, I still cannot fully explain what happened on that morning.

The early, hazy morning lights were just appearing on the horizon when I arrived on the intersection where Highway E42 meets Highway E411. I moved over to the right lane in order to join E411, which would take me to Luxembourg and from there to Strasbourg. A few kilometers down E411, closer to the exit towards the city of Namur, is the most-tricky part of this highway, because there are very steep slopes of ravines close to the tarmac on both sides of the road.

I was very much concentrating on driving safely through this stretch of the road when I saw a truck-trailer combination hanging dangerously with the cabin facing downwards into the ravine and the wheels of the trailer hanging in the air, wedged between the guard rails over the viaduct that lined this part of the road.

The moment I saw this accident, it felt as if time stood still in my mind. Everything I observed about this accident looked exactly like what I had seen in my dreams the night before. Even the trees where the cabin had smashed through on its way down, the way the truck was hanging precariously, and the rocks on the sides of the road looked the same.

Suddenly, I realized I was the first person to witness this accident, because there was no other car or truck in the vicinity in my direction of the highway at that time. I tried to stop, but the shoulder on this part of the road appeared to be too narrow for a truck to stop. However, with my hazard lights flashing, and my heart beating wildly, I managed to press 112-emergency services on my handset to report what I saw and continued on my way.

After driving through the difficult part of this highway, made up mostly of very high hills and deep valleys, my hands started shaking vigorously, and sweat broke out all over my body. I knew I had to get to a parking lot fast before I lost control. Luckily, I found one very soon and stopped to digest what I had just witnessed.

It was then it occurred to me that the dream I'd had the night before was a revelation of this accident. The two dogs I thought I had killed early that morning forced me to stop for almost twenty minutes on the other highway. It was meant to save me from this accident, which surely would have involved me—in fact, those twenty minutes saved my life.

Then and there it dawned on me that God had been communicating with me, He had been trying to get me to pay attention to what He wanted me to know, and He had been reaching out to me through dreams and now through signs and wonders. As soon as I came to this conclusion, I became very calm, and it felt as if someone I could not see was sitting there with me in my truck.

I prayed and thanked God for protecting me and for revealing to me what was to be. For, twice I experienced special dreams—first in Africa when I was ten years old and now on the highways of Western Europe. I promised that from then on, I was going to do His will, listen to His voice, and follow His instructions. And that prayer marked the beginning of this special relationship that I value more than anything else in my life up until this very day.

After this incident, I fully embraced the habit of praying and reading the Bible every day, and I would pray for clarity and understanding in every area of my life. I couldn't help but notice the subtle positive changes in my behavior. It was as if I became a different person. Miracles and kindness that I never expected from anyone or from anywhere began to show up regularly in my life. In fact, strangers would physically approach me just to talk about anything bothering them, and a few of my colleagues wanted to know what I was doing differently.

Many years have passed since then, and I am still using the Bible to know more about God, because this is a gradual process and a way of life. I have learned that anyone can communicate with God, but there are certain steps you must take to be certain that you are communicating with Him:

- You must understand that God is Spirit. Therefore, you must communicate with Him spiritually. You must choose consciously to stop doing things that will sabotage your spiritual awareness, you must control your emotions of anger, jealousy, and fear, and you must avoid loose talk and violence. If you cannot hold these weaknesses in check, I would suggest that you pray and ask for help. He will help you because He wants you to be clean—especially spiritually clean—to the extent that you understand that He is telling you things that He wants you to know, and He is providing answers to your questions. God always begins to build relationship with us by changing us from the inside out, because all the filth inside must be wiped clean.
- You must believe in God. The best way to know about God is by reading the Bible, because the Bible describes in detail the personality of God and the origins of life—including your life.

Recognize this and start from there. Use this knowledge and you will find yourself drawing close to God.

- Begin at once to listen. Be humble, be grateful, and obey. Let God know through your actions that you are ready to receive information. If He sees this, God will use the best channel suitable to your spiritual DNA to communicate with you. If it happens that you are not aware the first time, He will send this information time and time again until you get it. This means that He will sharpen your intuition, and somehow you will begin to see things differently from how you used to.

And to reassure us that He wants to communicate with us, He said these words in Jeremiah 33:3 (ESV):

Call to Me and I will answer you, and will tell you great and hidden things that you have not known.

CHAPTER TEN

COMMUNICATE THROUGH PRAYER

Prayer is the master key that unlocks all the doors of the universe.

There is considerable evidence to show that there is a tremendous power contained in a sincere and honest prayer to God. And prayer is by far greater than any type of mental therapy. Therefore, it is very important for everyone to know how to pray and understand that prayer is the best way to communicate with God.

Talking to God means communicating with Him through spiritual, personal, and often private means, and anyone can do this. Although many religions and popular opinions are propagating ideas that make prayer seem difficult and complicated, it doesn't have to be, because no matter your spiritual or religious preference, you can choose to use prayer simply to connect and talk to God.

However, it would be wise to consider what prayer can do for you before you embark on this endeavor. In fact, it is not wrong to be selfish or even to ask, "What's in it for me?" It is certainly not wrong to ponder whether it does any good. To understand this better, you must remember that in the Scriptures, even a most faithful man, Job, once pondered, in Job 9:16, "If I called and He answered me, I would not believe that He was listening to my voice."

The Bible proves certainly that God really does listen to prayer, but to get an answer we must pray in the right way and for the proper things, for in this way He will pay attention. That is why Psalm 145:18 confirms, "The LORD is near to all who call upon Him, to all who call upon Him in truth."

Now that we know the Bible confirms that God listens to our prayers, let us examine what we can expect when we make prayer a part of our lives, and let us consider some of the benefits of praying.

Peace of mind. In this present system of things—meaning the way of life on earth as we know it today—we are bombarded with problems and challenges, and because of this, many people are overwhelmed with worry and anxiety. It is in this kind of situation that prayer comes in handy.

We can receive a clear and calm feeling from prayer to gain a measure of tranquility when we pour out our worries and concerns to God, and by doing this we are helped to see that maybe the problem is not as serious as we make it to be. That is why the Bible encourages us to "pray without ceasing" at times like these, to "let your requests be made known to God."

The Bible further assures us in Philippians 4:7 that if we turn to God in prayer, "The peace of God, which surpasses all understanding, will guard your hearts and minds through Christ Jesus."

This shows that God does not want us to face our problems alone. Rather, He encourages us to pray for help, and I can assure you that countless people all over the world have experienced this peace of mind after prayer.

Comfort. When you are facing extreme stress from, perhaps, life-threatening or tragic circumstances, praying to God can bring immense relief. Even though the problems might seem bigger than you can carry, once you pray about them you are bound to feel relieved, as if you have received the power to endure. And prayer has the power to uplift you this way—that is why the Bible says that He "comforts us in all our tribulation."

Having used prayer many times to overcome difficulties, I would suggest that everyone should rely on prayer, especially in hard times, because it helps you to know that you are not alone—you have told someone who has the means to help you and is assuring you there is no cause for alarm, and everything is going to be alright.

Moreover, to show us that there is always a standby comfort coming from God, the Scriptures tell us in Second Corinthians 1:3–4: "Blessed be the God and Father of our Lord Jesus Christ, the Father of mercies and God of all comfort, who comforts us in all our tribulation, that we may be able to comfort those who are in any trouble, with the comfort with which we ourselves are comforted by God." This means we are granted favor to overcome and comforted to endure anything life throws at us when we pray.

Shielding from temptation. By praying, we are also helped to avoid temptation; for this reason, the Bible tells us to "pray, lest you enter into temptation."[51]

---

51   Mark 14:38.

Repentance. Through prayer, we show repentance and ask for forgiveness for our sins. The Bible states clearly in Second Chronicles 7:14:

> If My people who are called by My name will humble themselves, and pray and seek My face, and turn from their wicked ways, then I will hear from heaven, and will forgive their sin and heal their land.

The Bible text above shows that repentance and forgiveness can be achieved through prayer, for there is nothing to lose but very much to gain when we pray.

GUIDANCE TO MAKE WISE DECISIONS

When I look back on my life in the last twenty-three years, I realize that I am where I am today, supported by the good health I enjoy and with all the blessings in my life—and I am favored to write this book—because of my prayers to God at every stage of my journey.

Therefore, I am using this opportunity to thank God for all that He has done for me. I will also add that I am a living testimony of what you can achieve if you pray to God for guidance to make the right decisions.

I will never forget that I was a stowaway who hid in a ship that after many days at sea arrived in the Port of Rotterdam. I will always remember how miserable and how terribly alone I felt when I climbed out of my hiding place in that ship and made my way out of that area of the harbor. I recall that at some point I thought I had made a very big mistake—that I was daring fate, and I was going to suffer seriously for taking such a risk.

Nevertheless, I have come a long way since then, and I owe it all to the constant prayers I was praying to God to help me find my way. I am certain that God heard my prayers—or else, how could He have sent an angel to help me on my way the very first day I arrived in the Netherlands? For, that is what I choose to call the lady who helped me on that very first day.

It is in my testimony today: I am using my own words and humble ability to encourage anyone reading this book to put your trust and faith in God, because I am sure that if He can do such remarkable things for me, He will certainly do them for you as well.

Since 2003, I have been making my living as a truck driver. I love what I do, but in 2017 I noticed I was beginning to feel weary and restless, and I was no longer happy being on the road all the time.

But although I would love to do other jobs, I could not think of anything else to do, as I have been a trucker for a long time, and I do not have the money, time, and aptitude to go back to school to be trained in another sector of the economy. This would mean starting all over again, and it looked like a more difficult prospect than always being on the road.

So, I was confronted with a dilemma that was gradually welling up inside me. For the first time in years, I developed stress and anxiety and constant worry that I was going to make a terrible mistake from lack of concentration, which in driving may result in disastrous consequences. This made my situation even worse.

I do remember that one day during this period, I was traveling from Belgium back to Holland. The truck was cruising effortlessly along the E313 highway, approaching the Antwerp Ring, when suddenly out of nowhere, just about two hundred meters in front of me was a halted traffic jam that seemed like it was not going anywhere soon. I stepped on the brakes, screeching with overwhelmed brakes and tires, and I barely managed to stop the truck behind a family car in front of me.

It happened because I was so preoccupied with my worries that I had forgotten I was approaching a very busy section of the highway with a forty-ton truck on cruise control doing eighty-five kilometers per hour. I was very much shaken and terrified of what would have happened if I had not been able to bring the truck to a stop.

When I got back to Holland, I asked my boss for a one-week holiday, because I realized I was becoming a risk to other road users, and I needed some time away from work to clear my head, reassess my situation, and consider my options.

However, at this stage in my life, I had already developed an unshakeable belief in God. I could not make any major decision without seeking His help and direction. I knew that First John 5:14 says, "This is the confidence that we have in Him, that if we ask anything according to His will, He hears us." Because I understood that this decision would permanently affect not only me but my loved ones, I knew it was time to ask God to reveal to me what to do.

I do remember that during this period I was praying constantly, especially during those nights when I could not sleep due to anxiety. I prayed to God to reveal to me the gifts He bestowed on me when I was born as His child into this world. I felt that driving could not be the only thing I was good at. Therefore, I asked specifically that He show me the gift that is most suited to my personality and the one that could most benefit others as well.

I reminded God that it is written in His holy book in James 1:5: "If any of you lacks wisdom, let him ask of God, who gives to all liberally and without reproach, and it will be given to him."

After praying, I got the feeling that I had just submitted my application for a very important job to someone who had not only the means to help me but also the willingness to teach me. I felt so comforted that I left it at that, and the following week I reported back for duty—back on the roads again with a clear mind, as if nothing had happened.

Sometime the following week after I had gone back to work, I dreamed that I was sent back to a country in Africa as a reporter to investigate the case of a missing aid worker of a foreign NGO. And in this dream, I was tracing his movements, asking people along the way who had seen him. I was following their directions when I arrived at the market in the center of the town where I was born.

When I got to this point in the dream, I woke up only to discover that I was sleeping in my truck in a parking lot somewhere beside a major highway in Europe. I tried to make sense of what I had dreamed, but I could not, so I went back to sleep. And during this period, I had several dreams where I was doing some sort of writing at one time or the other, yet I could not make the connection.

After this phase, in the following months, I began to find myself in dreams where it would appear I was seeing a part of a film, and in the middle of the film, I would wake to discover I had been dreaming. And in one dream, I was with many people in a hall, and I was invited up to the podium to make a speech because of what I had written. But no matter how much I tried to understand what was happening to me, I still could not make any sense of it.

At some point during that year, I stopped paying attention to my dreams and began to accept them as my nightly routine. Gradually, the frequency of the dreams trickled down to one or two times a month, and finally, I did not have any dreams of that kind anymore—and to my surprise, I was no longer aware of when I'd had the last one, nor could I remember that I had prayed to God to show me what to do.

Meanwhile, I resigned from my job and found employment with another company, and within six months I'd resigned again and joined another company, as I could no longer find the job satisfaction I used to derive from my work.

Between 2017 and 2018, I must have worked for about six different transport companies before I finally settled for a company in Antwerp-Belgium that specializes in the transport of hazardous chemicals in the form of cryogen gases loaded in refrigerated tanks mounted on trailers. I must admit that I loved the challenges posed by that kind of work because it was a specialized kind of transport.

For a while, I was contented with this job because I was no longer driving all over the place in Europe. Rather, my area of operation was within the countries of Belgium, Netherlands, and Luxembourg, or Benelux, in regional parlance. Moreover, I only slept two or three nights a week in the truck instead of living almost the whole time in the truck.

I started working with this company in February 2018, and about six months later, I was sent to a chemical factory in Luxembourg to do a delivery. By the time I finished there, it was already late, so I had to spend the night on the road in my truck.

On this very night, I had a dream so unique that I could not ignore or dismiss it like I had done with the previous ones. I dreamed that someone gave me a plant and I planted it on a piece of ground, and I gathered some soil around this plant and proceeded to water it.

After giving water to this plant, it began to grow right in front of my eyes. As I continued watching, it grew into a big, tall tree, and it began to spread and multiply into several trees that covered the whole area as far as the eye could see. It transformed into a forest of high trees that seemed to have a continuous layer of green foliage.

When I looked up, I saw all kinds of birds with beautiful plumage settling at the very top branches of the trees in every direction. Looking down, I noticed men and women, young and old, and people from different backgrounds, from all walks of life, both white and black and every color of mankind together, gathering in small groups and resting under the shade of the trees. As I continued looking, I thought to myself that every one of them looked happy to be in that place with the others. But why was I alone, standing apart from them? As I took a step to join them, I woke up and realized I had been dreaming.

As I became fully awake, I noticed I had a smile on my face, and it took me a while to realize that I was asleep in my truck. I was excited for no reason, and I could not go back to sleep. So, I prayed to God to reveal the meaning of this dream to me.

I kept thinking about this dream the whole day on my way back to the base, and this time I knew someone was truly sending me a message—a message that would probably change my life. I had learned to put my faith in God, so I was sure that very soon something must happen to give me a hint of what was coming my way.

As it turned out, I did not receive any sign with regards to the meaning of that dream as quickly as I hoped. Rather, I began to dream regularly about writing and being in situations where I was involved in writing in different environments other than driving. Due to the volume of the material I was receiving in my dreams, I bought an exercise book and began to write them down with dates and times of the dreams so as not to forget.

To date, I have written down many remarkable stories I have received in my dreams, because I regard all of them as messages that will be revealed to me at the appropriate time. But something strange was happening to me, and even to this day, I cannot find the right words to describe what it was.

I can only assume that it started with my writing down the things I was dreaming about. From then onwards, I developed the habit of writing. I even began to watch YouTube videos and tutorials to learn tips on how to be a good writer, and any little opportunity I had was used for writing on just about any topic that caught my fancy.

The urge to write was so strong that I would be formulating topics and writing them in my head while busy with driving. It was as if I were under the influence of a bad habit I could not control.

Sometime during this period, toward the end of 2018, just a few weeks before Christmas, I went with my truck to our company garage to replace the air filter. While waiting for the mechanic to finish the replacement, I was approached by a colleague who was there also. After exchanging greetings, he asked me if I had taken a vacation that year and I told him no.

He asked me if I was going to take a few days off during this period. I was surprised by his question, but instead of telling him that I would prefer to take a few days off, I blurted out to him that I was going to resign next year—that I was tired of being on the road all the time.

I felt bad as soon as the words left my mouth, because it was not in my character to talk in such a flippant manner. It felt as if someone were talking through me. When he asked what I was going to do next if I stopped driving, I told him without hesitation that I was going to be a writer.

He seemed surprised when I told him this. Nonetheless, he wished me luck and walked away. But I was even more surprised at myself because I had never thought seriously about becoming a writer before this time. However, deep down I knew I had finally admitted what I had been afraid to accept as inevitable, and in that moment, I realized that this was the answer I had been waiting for and this was the meaning of all the dreams I had been having all that time.

On Friday evening, I was driving back to Holland from Belgium in my personal car as I always did every weekend, because even though I was employed in Belgium during this period, I was still living in Holland. But on this evening, when I arrived at my street, instead of driving straight into my own parking lot in front of my house, I drove slowly past, preoccupied and unaware of the vicinity. I heard a voice clearly speak to me, saying, "This is where you lived when you wrote your first book."

At first, I could not believe what I had just heard, and I thought maybe there was someone in the car with me. I stared at the passenger seat beside me, but there was no one—only me in the car, but before

I realized what had just happened to me, I had driven way past my house, almost to the end of the street. It was so unreal because I had never written a book in my life—moreover, I was still living in that house, so how could this be?

I felt goose bumps all over my body. I stopped, turned the car around, and drove back to my house. When I stepped into my living room, I sat down on the sofa in my familiar surroundings and thought for a while about what had just happened and about all the surreal writing experiences I had been having lately.

It was now very clear to me that God had used many channels to tell me that I was going to write a book. I remembered at once that it is written in the Scriptures in Matthew 7:7, "Ask, and it will be given to you; seek, and you will find; knock, and it will be opened to you." Finally, I got the message. "God has answered my prayer." At last, I remembered I had asked Him to reveal to me the gift He had bestowed on me when I was born into this world as His child.

That night, in my prayer to God, I thanked Him for giving me this gift and for revealing it to me. I promised Him I was going to use this gift to worship Him and let people know how great their lives will be if they put their faith and trust in God, the Giver of all gifts. I also promised to use my writing to help as many people as possible.

After the Christmas holidays in January 2019, I did not resign immediately. Rather, I went back to work in Belgium because I needed to save enough money to live on and support my family while writing my first book. And I continued working up until December, when I submitted my resignation letter. However, because of the terms of my contract, I was obliged to work till the end of January 2020.

After my resignation, I tried to start writing immediately, but I could not. Even though I had the topic ready to go, I realized that I was afraid to start. I was afraid that people would not like my book. I was afraid that if people found out that I have no degree from any university or that I am not highly educated, they would think I am a fraud. In fact, I was afraid of everything that could go wrong.

What bothered me most was the fact that I had no degree whatsoever from any higher institution. I only have a diploma in Transport and Logistics, which is the highest educational requirement for my former profession. I thought that writing a book and publishing it was only reserved for the highly educated, but little did I know how wrong I was at that time.

After hanging around for one month doing nothing, I considered going back to driving trucks again. Then one night, I was so restless I could neither relax nor fall sleep, and in the middle of the night, for no reason at all, I picked up my mobile phone and accidentally opened my Facebook page.

To my surprise, the first thing I saw posted on my wall by a friend were these words by Albert Einstein: "Education…is not the learning of many facts, but the training of the mind to think."

I thought about what I had just read for a while, and then the meaning of his words hit me, and I felt as if I had just received a massive dose of adrenalin. I could no longer continue to lie in bed, waiting to fall asleep, so I went downstairs to the bureau where I placed my laptop, opened it, and started writing.

I wrote the whole night until the following day, only stopping when I needed to use the WC. I noticed that when I was writing everything stood still, and I felt like I was living in another time zone. The ideas kept coming to me in successive relays in a back-to-back manner that brought the words forth before the next and the next hit me.

It took me six weeks to finish writing my first book, entitled, *The Ignorance of Racism*, and one week to go over it thoroughly and edit it. When I was done, I contacted three publishing companies in Holland to publish my work, but they all turned it down because it was not written in Dutch.

I was disappointed with the rejections, but by then, I had learned how to handle the unhappiness caused by discouragements. I remembered that it is written in the Scriptures, in Proverbs 3:5–6, "Trust in the LORD with all your heart, and lean not on your own understanding; in all your ways acknowledge Him, and He shall direct your paths."

Because I had developed the faith that if I ask for help from God, He will send it, I prayed for someone—a publishing company—to actually read my manuscript and make up their mind to publish it. Further, I prayed that the next publishing company I contacted would be the one to publish my book.

And so, it happened exactly. The following day I searched online, and the first publishing company I came across was based in the United Kingdom. I contacted them and sent my manuscript of *The Ignorance of Racism* to them, and after three months, I received a reply from them informing me that they would be glad to publish my work. They even stated why they had agreed to publish my work. I have decided to include part of their letter in this book to show what will happen if you put your trust and faith in God.

In late February 2021, I received an email from a publishing company in the United Kingdom with the subject line, RE: "The Ignorance of Racism."

Dear Mr. Lalluk,

Your manuscript was brought to our attention at the latest Editorial Board meeting when we discussed the potential of its publication. Having read all the reports and taken note of the Editors' opinions we can confidently state that your work was found to be a most absorbing and intriguing work, very well written, that will undoubtedly captivate a wide audience.

The Board was very pleased with the sophisticated narrative and a most compelling plot, part memoir and part essay, exploring very strong topics. We believe your work is very well-conceived and developed, allowing the readers to open themselves to awareness and understanding. "The Ignorance of Racism" is a well-written and researched work worthy of attention, and we believe it would have a place in the market.

This letter was signed by three members of the Board of Editors of the Publishing Company.

NOTICE!!!

If you are wondering the relevance of this letter to this book, I would prefer to put it in a manner that is unambiguously explicit and direct—that I am an ordinary truck driver—I have never attended any university, and I do not know anyone personally who is a writer or a publisher. I am a writer today because I prayed to God to reveal to me the gift, He bestowed on me when I was born into this world as His child.

Therefore, if you are facing difficulty in your attempt to solve a problem or in your attempt to achieve any goal, I would suggest that you pray to God and ask for help. I am one hundred percent sure that God will provide all the help you need to succeed.

Finally, I would remind you that it is also written in the Scriptures, "You do not have because you do not ask."[52] For, the moment you ask is the moment you start receiving. I strongly believe that God is doing it for me every day, and He is ready to do it for you if you ask. So, why not ask right now? Please don't wait.

---

[52]   James 4:2.

CHAPTER ELEVEN

ASK AND RECEIVE

And all things, whatsoever ye shall ask in prayer, believing, ye shall receive. (Matthew 21:22 KJV)

M illions of people all over the world want millions of things. While many people receive what they want, many do not receive. So, why do some receive and others not? Maybe the answer lies in the manner in which they seek what they want, or maybe the way they ask, or what they're asking for, or it could be in their faith that they will or will not receive if they ask.

In order to fully understand the concept of asking and receiving, it would be good to remember that even though you may receive a gift from someone at one time or the other without asking, it is not the same as receiving what you really want or need. To receive what you want, you must ask, and to receive what you need, you must seek. And no matter which option you choose, it is you who must make the first move.

Because this is an integral part of human nature, the Scriptures devote many verses from the Old Testament and the New Testament to highlighting the importance of asking and receiving.

For example, it is written in Jeremiah 29:11–13 (ESV), "For I know the plans I have for you, declares the LORD, plans for welfare and not for evil, to give you a future and a hope. Then you will call upon Me and come and pray to Me, and I will hear you. You will seek Me and find Me, when you seek Me with all your heart."

Because Jesus understands how important this issue is to mankind, He said in John 16:24, "Until now you have asked nothing in My name. Ask, and you will receive, that your joy may be full." Jesus is addressing not only His first twelve disciples in this Bible verse—He is also encouraging you and me and all of mankind to ask in His name. He is telling us to ask in His name. This means asking based on His authority, which involves asking according to the will of God.

It also means that the will of God is what Jesus always does, and if we ask according to the will of God, He hears us. Therefore, our requests must be in alignment with the will of God to be granted. It sounds so simple—ask and you shall receive—but what if what you ask for is not good for you? Or what if what you want at that time may hurt other people or goes against the will of God?

Many times, what people want is not what they need. So, if what people want is not in God's will, then they really shouldn't receive it. This is because God knows what is good for us. Therefore, even though He says yes many times to our requests, He will also say no to selfish and foolish requests, no matter how much we want them.

Because of this, it would be wise to remember before you ask that this is not a blanket promise with no conditions, for God is under no obligation to give us what we ask for. But on the other hand, Jesus is reassuring us that if we ask in His name, according to how He asks from His father, that God will not fail to give His children good things. What we ask for must be in agreement with God's advantageous gifts to us, and never will He give us bad or harmful gifts. To elaborate more on the right way to ask, Jesus said in Matthew 7:9–11:

> What man is there among you who, if his son asks for bread, will give him a stone? Or if he asks for a fish, will he give him a serpent? If you then, being evil, know how to give good gifts to your children, how much more will your Father who is in heaven give good things to those who ask Him!

By this statement, Jesus is confirming that the promise of asking and receiving according to God's will, can never disappoint. There is no chance of what we ask for not being in God's will if we seek to know Him and if we seek His kingdom and righteousness first, before asking, because He promises to supply all our needs accordingly.

Certainly, when we truly seek that God's will be accomplished on earth and when we desire to do things that bring Him glory, He is eager to give us anything we ask. This is because what we ask for will be with an understanding of what is good in God's eyes, made possible through our desire to cultivate good and to do good.

In order to ask and receive always, it would be good to understand why Jesus instructs us to ask in His name. He wants us to develop a close relationship with His Father, just as He Himself has a close relationship with God. Having a close relationship with God helps us to develop faith and belief that when we ask from Him, we will receive without fail only the good things from Him.

It is a continuous process to stay in an ongoing relationship with God. So, it is necessary to ask and continue asking, because when our initial motive is wrong, God will not give us the answer to a whim of ours that emanates from wrong thinking. But as we keep on asking, we are corrected to think the right way, and then what we want gets molded into what is really good for us.

Therefore, it is very important that we keep on asking, and if the answer is yes, be grateful and keep on communicating with God. If the answer is no, keep on asking until you either receive what you want or you receive the wisdom about why you didn't get it. Most of all, keep your supply lines to God open and keep loving your Heavenly Father by obeying Him and communicating with Him.

SOMETIMES WE ASK FOR ONE THING BUT RECEIVE ANOTHER

Many times, we ask for something and receive it. But other times, we do not receive, or we receive something different from what we asked for. This simply means that the process of asking contains learning and growing in wisdom to understand first that in God you have all you need and all your source. You must learn to trust that He knows what you really need according to His priorities for you.

To understand this better, it would be helpful to consider the story of Solomon in First Kings, starting from chapter 3. Here the Bible narrates how Solomon asked God for a discerning heart to rule his people and to distinguish between right and wrong. Solomon understood that God is the source of knowledge, and so He was pleased that Solomon asked for wisdom and understanding instead of fleeting things like wealth or honor.

Because of this honest request, God gave Solomon not only a very wise heart but also the wealth and honor he did not ask for. So,

Solomon asked for the best thing he needed to be a good ruler and received other blessings as well.

We must never forget that God has already provided the best things in life necessary for us to have a good life—such things as the air we breathe, the sun, the water, the seasons, and the soil from which we grow our food. He will give us everything we need—and besides, what we need is more important than what we want.

It is better to ask for things from God through prayer, but we must base our prayer and request on the fact that the most important things we need we have received already and continue to receive daily. That is why Deuteronomy 28:11–13 assures us that:

> The LORD will grant you plenty of goods, in the fruit of your body, in the increase of your livestock, and in the produce of your ground, in the land of which the LORD swore to your fathers to give you. The LORD will open to you His good treasure, the heavens, to give the rain to your land in its season, and to bless all the work of your hand. You shall lend to many nations, but you shall not borrow. And the LORD will make you the head and not the tail; you shall be above only, and not be beneath, if you heed the commandments of the LORD your God, which I command you today, and are careful to observe them.

In other words, the Scriptures are telling us to pay attention to the words of God, to understand that to ask and receive is not a one-time agreement like ordering something from Amazon.com or Alibaba.com or any other online shop only when we need it.

Rather, we are encouraged to continue in our relationship with God, to know His will and ask accordingly. It may simply mean learning and growing in wisdom and thereby developing the faith and understanding that when we ask from God, He will surely deliver.

Moreover, it is proven that the more we learn about God, the more we have faith in Him, and faith plays a very important role in receiving. That is why in the Bible, Mark 11:22–24 counsels us to develop the unshakeable faith of Jesus, which was always on display. This Bible verse declares:

> So Jesus answered and said to them, "Have faith in God. For assuredly, I say to you, whoever says to this mountain, 'Be removed and be cast into the sea,' and does not doubt in his heart, but believes that those things he says will be done, he will have whatever he says. Therefore, I say to you, whatever things you ask when you pray, believe that you receive them, and you will have them."

Moreover, having faith in God helps to remove the corrupt human factors of doubt and manipulations—God must not be doubted or manipulated—and to replace them with the unquestionable belief acceding to God's plan as the best of the best for us.

Now that you are equipped with this knowledge, you should start asking from God immediately. Do not delay, for many people fail before they even begin because they fail to ask for what they want.

CHAPTER TWELVE

WATCH OUT FOR SIGNS

> I thought it good to declare the signs and wonders that the Most
> High God has worked for me. (Daniel 4:2)

T he Bible has assured us through many verses that miraculous signs will accompany those who put their faith in Jesus Christ. There are numerous evidence confirming that signs and wonders have followed those who believe in God, both in the past and in our present day.

Anyone can receive miraculous signs in their life, because they are a gift from God and are not limited or determined by how we look or who we are or our position in society. But there is a proven way to witness the power of God and His signs and wonders in your life. It is by spending time with God that you become so intimate that His wish becomes your wish.

In order to clarify this notion of spending time with God, the Bible says in James 4:8:

> Draw near to God and He will draw near to you. Cleanse your
> hands, you sinners; and purify your hearts, you double-minded.

However, this does not mean you should go seeking for signs and wonders. Rather, you must watch out for them in your life and allow them to guide you in making your decisions. I have come to believe that since I started reading the Bible and using it to draw nearer to God, it has enabled me to communicate with God in a way that I never would have imagined possible.

I am acutely aware that before this time, I was always angry because there was so much disparity in this world. I was quick to point fingers and pass judgement and even blame other people whom I felt were responsible one way or another. But studying the Scriptures has helped me to understand that all of mankind is floating and drifting on this current of imperfection, and the failure of one (Adam) led to the failure of all.

I am now fully aware that even though it might be possible for many people to develop a close relationship with God as a congregation of like-minded persons, it is mostly not a group thing. On the contrary, it is something best achieved on an individual basis because it requires personal sacrifice, openness, and willingness to do away with certain flaws, beliefs, and attitudes that control our personal behaviors in the present world system of things.

For example, the Bible will help you to understand that God does not see humans as White or Black or Mixed or Yellow or Green or Brown. Neither does He see us as Americans, Africans, Europeans, or Asians. And God has no preference for any religion over the other, because most of them are false. In fact, He wants to do away with all false religions. Rather, He is concerned about the true religion—that is why He made sure that the Bible was written under His inspiration.

I am a strong believer in God and His Son Jesus Christ, and because of my faith, I am fervently praying that His will be done on earth as it is done in heaven and His kingdom be established on earth under the rulership of Jesus as king.

Even though Christianity lays claim to the Bible, it does not mean that people of other faiths cannot use the Bible to get to know God. The Bible is available to all people, crossing all boundaries. The closer you draw to God, the more you will understand that the human, divisive way of carving out territories of land and sea and air space and labelling them as one country or the other is wrong and has nothing to do with religion or God.

Because of my determination to hold on to my spiritual principles in order to do His will, I have intentionally refrained from mentioning any country as my place of origin or place of birth. However, I am indebted to the government of the Netherlands for their kind gesture toward me, and only the authorities reserve the right to tell where I come from to any curious inquirer. I will always consider myself favored because when I arrived in the Netherlands, the people and the authorities gave me a place to live among them to develop and pursue this knowledge that has transformed my life into what it is today. I am thankful to many people that accepted me for who I am and not for how I look or where I come from.

While I am conscious of divisions, I no longer consider myself different from any other person. I do not view myself as a citizen of any particular country or any particular race. This does not mean that I am not aware of the physical features that differentiate me from others. Rather, I am privileged and grateful to know that there are more than seven billion people on earth right now and we are one enormous human family, and every day I look forward to meeting one or two of my newfound brothers and sisters.

I would recommend that you start using the Bible to understand God's plan for you and develop a thought pattern that will flush out the corrupt influences of the world that are pulling the strings in your day-to-day mindset to block the manifestation of signs and wonders in your life. If you choose to do this, you will find out that signs and wonders are God's supernatural, miraculous power breaking into the natural world of mankind and doing what is impossible by natural physical laws and understanding. The most rewarding way to witness the power of God in your life is by using the Bible to spend quality time with Jesus and develop intimacy that will enable you to walk as He walked.

In order to fully understand the benefit of this intimate relationship with Jesus, you ought to consider that in the Scriptures, Acts 4:13–14 describes the Apostles Peter and John as uneducated and untrained men, yet they developed boldness to speak and preach the Gospel, healed the sick, and performed signs and wonders beyond their standing and status in their society. And even the people in power marveled at the apostles' ability to do these things, only to realize that they had been with Jesus.

In my case, I am a truck driver, but signs have led me to become the writer I am today. Having finished writing my first book, *The Ignorance of Racism*, and while waiting for its publication, I went back to work as a truck driver. Sometime in April 2021, I dreamed that I was driving along the expressway and stopped on the shoulder of the road to ease myself. I stepped out of my car and walked toward the grass beside the roadway.

As I moved closer to the grass, I saw a very smooth stone lying on the grass in front of me, and when I bent down to pick it up, I saw another one lying in the grass further away from where I was standing. This stone lying further away from me was bigger in size and looked different from the first one, and I noticed it was partially covered with grass and mud.

So, instead of picking up the first stone that was very smooth, I picked up the second stone, and I observed that there were some words written on it in an alphabet I could not understand. It appeared to be quite a remarkable stone indeed because, while the first stone was very smooth and shiny, this other stone looked like something done by a craftsman. Suddenly, with this realization, I woke up from this dream, wondering what it was all about.

In the days following this dream, I kept thinking about the stones, all the time trying to figure out the meaning of the words written on the second stone. I know from past experience that trying to know the meaning behind any dream is a difficult thing, because a dream may be just a dream, or it could be a message, and it pops up out of nowhere unexpectedly.

Still, I am a strong believer that dreams, signs, and wonders can be supernatural acts and occurrences by which God demonstrates His omnipotence to miraculously reveal His intentions to us or communicate with us. Because of this, I prayed to God to reveal the meaning of this dream to me and let me know specifically if it was something I must do or something to watch out for.

After two months during which nothing happened in terms of any sign whatsoever, I stopped thinking about the dream entirely. Meanwhile, during this waiting period, I started writing another book. In order to find time to write, I resigned from my day job and found other employment as a night driver to have time during the day to write.

In this new job, my assignment was to pick up a loaded trailer from a logistic depot in the Dutch city of Roosendaal and take it to another depot in the city of Zwolle, about a one-and-a-half-hour drive. And after unloading, I would have to load again at the same depot for the trip back to my starting point.

However, on one of these nights, I was very tired, and I stopped for a thirty-minute break in a parking lot at Willemsbos, along Highway A28, close to the town of Nunspeet. After eating some snacks, I drifted off to sleep, and during this short sleep that lasted not longer than twenty minutes, I dreamed that I was at home writing a book on my computer, but I did not know the name or the subject matter.

Suddenly, for no reason at all, I abruptly woke up and realized I had been dreaming in my truck, and somehow, I was bothered that I was writing a book with no name. I thought, how is it possible? Nevertheless, I had a long journey before me, and I had to make sure to deliver these goods to the receiving depot before the night shift clocked out.

I checked the time and noticed it was three thirty in the morning. I drove out of the parking lot, and maybe two kilometers away from the parking lot, along a very wooded stretch of this highway, I heard a voice clearly say to me, *"King of Kings."* I thought I was hearing voices, so I continued looking at the passenger seat in the truck, but there was no one else in the truck—only me.

I kept looking on every side of the road ahead of me, but there was no other truck or any sign of another person close by at that time of the night. Then, out of nowhere, I heard the same voice again clearly and a bit louder, this time saying, "The name of the book is *King of Kings*." Instantly, I felt a cold chill over my face, and I had goose bumps all over my body.

I knew that this was the meaning of the dream, and in that moment, I understood that I would be writing a book titled *The King of Kings*. It was clear to me that those two dreams were connected, and I remembered I had asked God to specifically reveal the meaning of the dream about the stones to me. God had answered my prayers in a most personal way.

I stopped on the shoulder of the road and prayed, and I thanked God for His kindness in revealing things that are beyond my understanding. As soon as I finished praying, I felt as if my mind was open to all of God's creation and I was ready to receive knowledge beyond my comprehension, and almost immediately, ideas and plots and story lines began to flow into my mind from everywhere. I must have driven the hundred-and-fifty kilometers distance on autopilot before I noticed I was at the entrance of the depot of my stop point in Roosendaal.

Shortly thereafter, I stopped writing the other book I had been busy with before that time and started writing this book, *The King of Kings*. Even as I am writing these things down, I cannot fully explain how I came to be this way. However, I would testify that signs and wonders are special miracles that can happen to anyone—including you—and they signify that something miraculous is going on in your life and you need to pay attention.

God's signs and wonders are always intended to make people wonder about important things instead of being unaware of them. They are always in harmony with the Word of God and show that your prayers are heard, and that God is with you. It would be wise to consider them as immediate and powerful acts of God designed to reveal something or to reveal His character and purposes for us.

HOW DO SIGNS AND WONDERS WORK?

- Signs and wonders can work with or without faith by the recipient, even though faith helps you to realize it is meant for you.
- Signs and wonders can be verified by the recipient through prayer.
- Signs and wonders never contradict the Word of God.

However, I must conclude by stating that signs and wonders cannot be used to replace God in your life. Do not imagine that God Himself changes, for God is the master Miracle Worker, He is in control, and He is the one in charge of signs and wonders.

CHAPTER THIRTEEN

OBEDIENCE

> But the one who looks into the perfect law, the law of liberty, and perseveres, being no hearer who forgets but a doer who acts, he will be blessed in his doing. (James 1:25 ESV)

God has given so much to mankind that we should be grateful for. But above all, He has demonstrated His love for us, even after our forebears Adam and Eve disobeyed Him and changed the course of life He had planned for humans. He offered salvation to mankind by sacrificing His only begotten Son in order to fulfill His initial purpose for creating humans.

We must never forget that salvation is a free gift from God, with no strings attached, and we can do nothing to merit it. However, we can position ourselves to benefit from His generous salvation offer by submitting to His authority through obedience. We must understand that God is using the Bible to teach us spiritually and help us to be inspired and have the belief and trust that motivates us in turn to act in accordance with His desires and expectations for us. For, this is the real meaning of obedience.

In the Bible, the life and ways of Jesus show that obedience is the practical acceptance of the authority and will of God. He taught us that this means submitting to God, expressing that submission through actions, words, and thoughts. He proved that to be obedient to God means to be in agreement with God, and to be in agreement with God is to be in a position of power.

In order to understand how obedience to God can help humans to be successful and elevate them to a position of power, it would be wise to consider the real-life experience of the Israelites after they left Egypt en route to the land that God had promised to them.

This part of their history shows that when they listened and obeyed God, their journey was easy, and God protected them and provided for all their needs. But when they became obstinate, headstrong, and disobedient, they faced untold hardship. As a result of this stubbornness, the generation that started the journey from Egypt died on the road during the forty years which they wandered aimlessly, and they did not see the promised land because of their resistance to heed the Word of God.

Another good example to learn from is the story of Solomon, whom God loved so much that He blessed him with wisdom and stupendous wealth. The Bible narrative shows that when King Solomon obeyed God, listened to instructions from God, and carried out God's commandments, he was successful beyond his imagination. But when Solomon disobeyed God, married hundreds of women, and erected pagan altars for his wives' many gods within his kingdom, jealous kings and enemies from far and near were able to attack his kingdom and take away large chunks of his empire.

This was a painful learning experience for Solomon, to the extent that he wrote it in the Bible for future generations to learn from in Ecclesiastes 12:13–14, which says:

> Let us hear the conclusion of the whole matter: Fear God and keep His commandments, for this is man's all. For God will bring every work into judgment, including every secret thing, whether good or evil.

There are countless narratives in the Bible showing the benefits of obedience and the painful rewards of disobedience to God, but for the sake of those who have no knowledge of the Bible or the majority who consider the Word of God to be fiction or something not really relevant in the modern world of today, I would like to share the real-life example of a generally accepted way of life in the Netherlands. This example reflects the disappointing results of disobedience, when people choose not to live according to God's desire for us to keep our bodies and minds clean from all contaminations.

This accepted way of life is best described as the legal right and freedom of any consenting adult to use cannabis, or marijuana products, because of an open and permissive society that greatly emphasizes tolerance to do what you want with your life.

However, before I proceed, I must state that the use of cannabis and other addictive substances is a worldwide problem, and there is no government anywhere in the world that encourages people to indulge in the use of recreational drugs. But the difference is that while one might be cautioned or even arrested in other countries for possession of marijuana, in the Netherlands, you can walk into any coffee shop, buy your weed, and light up as much as you want without any harassment from the police or any law-enforcement authority.

Yet, lying in wait is *the green snake in the green grass.*

Every summer during the holiday season, people from all corners of the globe travel to the Netherlands to spend their holidays. While some of them are visiting to see the land and admire its numerous beaches, windmills, and waterways, the vast majority of them—especially the younger generation—come for the Dutch experience of smoking weed in the coffee shops of Amsterdam, Rotterdam, Maastricht, and other cities of Holland.

Many coffee shops are open from nine o'clock in the morning until late in the night, and if you are eighteen and above you have the right and freedom to walk into any of them and buy a few grams, a joint of cannabis, or any choice marijuana product and partake of this freedom by buzzing up and getting high.

Due to the popularity and lucrative aspects of this habit, many coffee-shop owners have developed various strains of this product designed to target the minds and feelings of their customers so as to get them hooked so they keep coming back for more. Some owners are very creative to the extent that they have come up with exotic and cheesy names to make an impression on the user. Therefore, do not be surprised to see such names as, "White Widow," "Black Widow," "Pink Lady," "Cush," "Blue Haze," "Sputnik," "Skunk," etc., on the advertising boards hanging in these coffee shops as popular products of the day.

Nevertheless, no matter what name they come up with, you have to be aware that you are buying weed, cannabis, marijuana, pot, Indian hemp, dagga, ganja—regardless of the numerous names used to popularize this product.

But, before you light up, it would be wise to know that cannabis has a spirit, just like alcohol, despite the physical dissimilarities. You must understand that this spirit will do your bidding at your first contact and would love to be your companion for as long as possible.

For example:

If you want to be mellow and view things in a haze, it will reward you instantly. And if you want to think deeply and contemplate any mental exercise, or even feel wistful and induce the fantasy that you are doing something worthwhile while doing nothing, you will be rewarded also.

If you happen to have lost your appetite and you wish to regain it, the spirit of marijuana will stimulate you to be hungry and give you what is referred to in smoking parlance as the "munchies." So also, those suffering from some form of neurotic or rheumatic pain might receive temporary relief from their pain after using marijuana—in this case, "medical marijuana."

If you choose to let your anger loose, get out of control, and—*God forbid*—go on a rampage, the spirit of marijuana will encourage you as well—and even if you are dead wrong, it will make you think you are damn right.

And for anyone prone to the feelings of self-consciousness and inability to act in a relaxed and natural way, this spirit of marijuana will help you to lose your inhibitions. In fact, it may twist your personality to become talkative, rumbustious, and obnoxious.

But, for those who are inclined to sit on their butts or lay about on the sofa watching television or playing video games all day, if they happen to smoke weed, this spirit will encourage them to be lazy, untidy, and dirty, with an appearance best described as slovenly. But on the other hand, I have also seen men smoke a "roach" during their lunch break and still go back to their jobs, operating million-dollar equipment without batting an eye.

This is what marijuana can do for you, because this spirit invoked by usage wants to be shown all the secret places of your mind. It wants to get you hooked to increase your daily dosage in order to take control of your personality, and the only way to do that is to give you the illusion that it can do wonders for you.

The spirit of marijuana is a tricky and unreliable companion to party with because after a period of association with this substance, after the holidays are over, you will notice that you have become addicted and dependent on it. You can no longer make any decision without consulting this spirit, and from the moment you wake up till you retire for the day, you are constantly manipulated and driven by your craven desire for his soundless nod of approval telling you that everything is going to be alright if you just light a joint.

Once your habit, purchased and sustained with your hard-earned money, is firmly in the grips of the spirit of marijuana, that spirit turns into a parasitic worm eating up all the sweet, juicy, and beautiful aspects of your personality and replacing them with worthless and unrecognizable chaff with little or no substance. Only then will you finally realize that you've been robbed of the ability to obey yourself, and it has become a struggle to give yourself a positive command and carry it out.

For instance, instead of using cannabis to chill and relax and be mellow as you used to do in the beginning, the spirit of this substance will no longer listen to you and provide the feeling you want. Rather, it will dictate that you smoke more and more to achieve that feeling, which will in turn cause you to be more and more stoned.

A majority of weed smokers understand that being stoned is not a good state to be in, because instead of feeling cool and relaxed, those good feelings are now replaced with a feeling of restlessness and sometimes headaches. Your eyes will be red and swollen, and you will have a racing heartbeat, coupled with the inability to focus and concentrate.

For those who have arrived at this stage of their relationship with marijuana, and if they are honest with themselves, they will notice that their temperament has been compromised and they are more and more inclined to be angry, edgy, agitated, and sometimes unreasonable and headstrong for no apparent reason or for the slightest of provocations.

There will be tell-tale evidence of early addiction, such as unkempt physical appearance, dirty-brown fingernails resulting from sticky tetrahydrocannabinol and nicotine tar deposits from tobacco mix, and a funky, pungent smell of stale marijuana clinging to you wherever you go. Some users may or may not be aware of this, but others smell it as soon as they come in contact with you.

You must accept that this is the new you, and you are now on your way to becoming that which you did not wish to be: an addict, or even lower—a junkie.

It is a well-known fact that not all cannabis users move on to using hard drugs, but most of those who are now at this stage of longtime association with weed are referred to as "pothead," or "weed head," because their world now revolves around being high all the time and because of their disposition toward this dominant spirit of addiction.

Many psychiatrists and medical doctors have concluded that because of this subtle and carefree view on soft drugs, alcohol, and prostitution such as we find in the Netherlands, many who become used to being intoxicated, high, and promiscuous most of the time move from smoking cannabis to the use of highly addictive and mind-bending substances, like amphetamines, heroin, crystal meth, crack cocaine, and cocaine. And some have descended even lower, to the level of sniffing turpentine or laughing gas in order to get extra high.

If you have descended to any of these levels and become hooked on any of these substances, you will observe that your life is spiraling out of control. Even if your spirit is willing to fight, your body and mind cannot mount any tangible resistance. You will also notice that you have become a mere figure of what you used to be.

For example:

If you used to dress nicely in the past, now you have made a U-turn from a fancy dresser to a shabby dresser. From that unimpressive image, you regress further, to wearing raggies and rag-na-rag. And because of your addiction, instead of waking up wanting to brush your teeth first thing in the morning, you prefer to get a fix to kick start your day, and from then onwards, your once-beautiful teeth gradually rot and become something to be ashamed of due to personal neglect.

Your wallet will be constantly robbed and left empty by this habit, and if you were once rich, money will be flowing away from you like a river rushing downhill. If you used to just get by before, you will sell all your valuable possessions and finally resort to begging or even sell your body and dignity to support this habit.

For anyone who is not incarcerated in any physical correctional institute but still has the freedom to do what he wants to do, I would say that these conditions described above are the lowest form of self-imposed mediocre existence that anybody could wish for themselves.

However, I would also caution that all is not lost for anyone in this position, because what goes into a man does not defile him—rather, what comes out of that man is what defiles him. And for this reason, it is possible to reverse this addiction that is keeping you down by using your God-given free will to choose a good life, pull yourself out of this sordid caricature of life, and choose the meaningful existence that is your birthright from God.

It is time to personally acknowledge that you chose the spirit of addiction and made it your reality. Maybe knowingly or maybe unknowingly, like most people in the world today, you considered the Bible and Word of God as fiction and irrelevant in the present system of things. So, if your reality has ruined your life, why not try "fiction"? I am suggesting from my personal experience that you try the Word of God, because my life now is a testimony to the healing power of God. I would unequivocally state that sometimes the only One you need to talk to is in heaven. I affirm that if you make up your mind right now to talk to God, He will listen and come to your aid. I will refer to Isaiah 41:13 to prove it. In this Bible verse, God says, "For I, the LORD your God, will hold your right hand, saying to you, 'Fear not, I will help you.'"

Therefore, if you are tired of your addiction and you want to regain control of your life, you must pray and ask God for help to overcome your addiction. You must start now—do not wait—never mind that you are high or intoxicated, for even if you are, as soon as you begin to pray you will be surprised to notice that your words are becoming coherent. And if they are coherent, that means you are becoming sober. And if you are sober, that means you are conscious that you are asking for help.

Please, continue in this manner, because this is your first win in this battle. As you keep on praying, despite your mental state, you will become more and more aware that you are making a request contrary to the feelings of your state of addiction. This awareness shows that your sobriety is slowly dominating the other feelings caused by addiction, because prayer and sobriety go hand in hand.

Now that you know this, the next step is to develop discipline to pray constantly, and your prayer should be more in the direction of asking God to help you to avoid temptation, especially to help you to keep away from your smoking friends and smoking and drinking environments. Please do not forget to ask for an uplifting habit to replace your habit of addiction so as not to leave any vacuum or empty space in your mind.

Begin immediately to read self-development books in conjunction with the Bible to expose your weaknesses so you can banish them once and for all and discover your hidden strengths, for this will give you a sense of purpose to develop a new willpower to have worthwhile goals to aim for and a picture of how and what you want yourself to be.

Never let a day go by without praying, as this will help you to believe that you are not alone. Moreover, it will convince you that someone is watching over you and you do not want to let this person down. After this, your next step is to make a promise to yourself to obey your own command to resist the compulsion to indulge in the weaknesses of your old habit.

The more you read daily and pray, you will begin to notice a tangible change in yourself and a significant distaste for your addiction. By this time, you will surely be aware that God is helping you with the strength to resist the temptations of your old habit. Therefore, thank God for His support and make the promise and commitment to obey Him and listen to Him, because you are now on your way to recovery.

You may still falter and succumb to your addiction, nevertheless, you are now aware that God is standing by to help you fight this spirit of addiction. As long as God is on your side, you are sure to overcome, but you must ask Him to help you because you are fighting a spirit that has the whole world in its grip.

In the Bible, the struggle against the spirit of addiction, along with other spirits, is portrayed. It is described in Ephesians 6:12, which says:

> For we do not wrestle against flesh and blood, but against principalities, against powers, against the rulers of the darkness of this age, against spiritual hosts of wickedness in the heavenly places.

However, we are not left empty-handed in this fight, because in Ephesians 6:13, we are advised:

> Therefore, take up the whole armor of God, that you may be able to withstand in the evil day, and having done all, to stand.

It very important to use the Bible to learn how to acquire help and power to overcome bad habits and addictions, but this does not mean reading the Bible only when you encounter problems. It is necessary to make it your habit to read the Bible daily in order to fully understand that obedience to God means to hear, to trust, to submit, to surrender to Him and His instructions, and to keep your body free from all contaminations.

> I beseech you therefore, brethren, by the mercies of God, that you present your bodies a living sacrifice, holy, acceptable to God, which is your reasonable service. And do not be conformed to this world, but be transformed by the renewing of your mind, that you may prove to yourselves what is good and acceptable and perfect will of God. (Romans 12:1–2)

This real-life picture of addiction, as can be witnessed in most parts of the world today, illustrates the damage done by disobedience to God. May it serve as a cautionary tale for those who may not have counted the cost of their actions when they go contrary to God's best plans for humanity.

BENEFITS OF OBEDIENCE TO GOD

1. Those who are obedient can walk with God.
2. Spiritual and physical blessings await all who are obedient to God.
3. Obedience positions you wherever you are to receive God's mercy and favor.

4. Obedience helps you to develop resistance against temptation and reinforces your trust in God, so you can know who He is for you.

Therefore, choose now to preserve your body and your mind as a holy temple of God and develop the habit of obedience to Him, because when you learn to obey God, you have found the route to prosperity.

WELCOME TO PROSPERITY

The word *prosperity* evokes happiness in every human being, because happiness and prosperity go hand in hand. Prospering means that you are successful, flourishing, and operating in a thriving condition— including in financial areas, goodwill from others, peace and well-being, opportunity, and good health.

Therefore, when you think about prosperity, you must understand that it is the birthright of all humans to be prosperous, even though man-made conditions have made it impossible for many to enjoy prosperity. Nonetheless, you ought to know that God's thoughts concerning your happiness and prosperity are much higher than you can imagine.

To fully understand how much God wants us to prosper, you have to consider that He created everything on earth and the universe before He created humans, and after that, He gave us dominion over all of these things to use and create prosperity for ourselves and for others.

For instance, just imagine the oceans and seas and the rivers and all the waterways and how prosperous they are, with the billions of aquatic living things that thrive in them—or the tropical rainforests and lush vegetation and greenery, with all the organisms that they contain.

You can also see prosperity when you look up to the heavens at night. You will see millions of stars in different shapes, forms, and sizes. Even in the animal kingdom, you will observe that they are created to prosper in their natural environments, and all of nature was designed by God to renew itself and regenerate to become even more prosperous.

All these examples are the different forms of prosperity in the mind of God, for even though they might appear huge and awesome in the eyes of humans, they are just a tangible fraction of the prosperity that God has in store for you if you are His child. This is because you are elected by God, and you were chosen before the foundation of the world to make use of all that is contained in the universe to prosper.

Therefore, prosperity is not something to be considered lightly in a small-minded way but something as huge as the universe, for the universe is the most perfect example of prosperity.

Be mindful that prosperity was not bestowed on us because of anything humans have done. Rather, it is given by God as an expression of His favor. It was His original design and intention to create us, to love us, and to choose us to bear His image and use all He left at our disposal to create prosperity. So, despite who we are or what we have done, we can reclaim God's favor in the form of prosperity from God.

Yes, you can reclaim your favor with God and embrace prosperity. However, in order to do that, you may have to start seeing prosperity from God's view, which means recognizing His desire to bless you and give you His peace, protection, and all conditions that bring you joy, pleasure, delight, sweetness, loveliness, and goodwill.

God wants you to succeed and thrive in a way that translates into having a measure of self-control, morality, and awareness of the well-being of others. This is the way to acquire favor from Him, and His favor will release great blessings, including prosperity, good health, opportunity, advancement, and goodwill from others.

When you begin to receive favor and blessing from God, others will recognize it and gravitate toward you. He can cause your circumstances to change in one day, no matter where you are in your life. Your story will be compared to that of Joseph in the Bible—who experienced God's favor and went from prison to palace—because there is nothing in life that can hold you down.

So, if you are ready to welcome prosperity, begin now to seek to transform your life and do the will of God, and you will receive the real prosperity that is in essence to be fully sufficient by God's provision and fully for others. And to confirm God's promise, Second Corinthians 9:8 says:

> And God is able to make all grace abound toward you, that you, always having all sufficiency in all things, may have an abundance for every good work.

Now, I ask you earnestly to get ready, be excited, and prepare yourself to receive new favor, blessing, prosperity, peace, and protection, because God is ready to release them toward you. For, it is His desire to give you only good things.

PART FOUR

OUR FATHER'S WILL

The Lord is not slack concerning His promise, as some count slackness, but is longsuffering toward us, not willing that any should perish but that all should come to repentance. (Second Peter 3:9)

Therefore, do not be unwise, but understand what the will of the Lord is. (Ephesians 5:17)

The most common stumbling block that keeps many people from doing the will of God is the inability to truly understand who God is. In order to know who God is, we must consider His nature, His character, and His work.

Therefore, the right questions to ask are, Who is God? What is God? How can we know that He is God?

CHAPTER FOURTEEN

WHO IS GOD?

T he fact of the existence of God is obvious and conspicuous both through creation and through the human conscience, which knows right from wrong; These are coupled with our given ability to reason with logic rather than looking to coincidence and happenstance.

On that note, we must reason correctly to define who God is, because a false definition of God is blasphemy and idolatry.

A good summary of the definition of God is that God is the Supreme Being, the Creator and Ruler of all that is, and the Self-Existent One, who is awesome and perfect in power, goodness, and wisdom. It is an indisputable fact that He has no beginning and will never have an end.

However, to have an accurate knowledge about God, we must consult the Bible, because "All Scripture is given by inspiration of God, and is profitable for doctrine, for reproof, for correction, for instruction in righteousness."[53] Moreover, the Bible has a unique record of historical accuracy, enduring preservation, and transparent translation.

Unsurprisingly, right on cue—the first appearance of God in the Bible is in the very first verse, Genesis 1:1. Here the Scripture says, "In

---

[53]   Second Timothy 3:16.

the beginning God created the heavens and the earth." Accordingly, the Bible never tries to prove the existence of God—rather, it assumes God's existence from the very beginning, before everything else.

The Bible even goes further to explain that no person has ever seen God, because He is Spirit. This means that He is a higher form of life than humans or any physical creature that lives on earth. For this reason, it is written in Exodus 33:20: "But He said, 'You cannot see My face; for no man shall see Me, and live!'"

Notwithstanding that no human has seen God physically, the Bible also informs us that we are created in the image of God. This is the only concrete evidence to show that among all that He created, only humans have the image and physical appearance that can be compared to the true physical embodiment of God.

It is therefore correct to say that God is "omnipresent"—that He is capable of being everywhere at the same time, and His presence encompasses the whole of the universe. There is no location where He does not inhabit, and He may choose to appear in any form that He wishes.

He is also "omnipotent." In other words, God has supreme power to do what He wants, and His power is infinite and limitless. But above all, God is "omniscient." He is all knowing and aware of the past, the present, and the future, and He knows all there is to know and all that can be known.

Truly, God is all of the above and much more than we can imagine as humans, but to know what He really looks like, we have to take into consideration all the physical attributes of His only begotten Son, Jesus Christ, who is described in Colossians 1:15 in such a manner to show that "He is the image of the invisible God, the firstborn over all creation."

Based on this insight from the Scriptures, it would not be blasphemous to say that if God were to choose to reveal Himself physically, then His Son, Jesus Christ, would bear the closest resemblance to Himself that humans would be honored to see, and two thousand years ago, many people were privileged to see Him. Nevertheless, despite the physical resemblance, we must not assume that Jesus and His Father are equal, for only the Father is omnipresent, omnipotent, and omniscient.

To show a clear distinction between Father and Son, the Bible says in John 1:18, "No one has seen God at any time. The only begotten Son, who is in the bosom of the Father, He has declared Him." Although He is greater than His Son in authority, He nevertheless shares all that He has with Him, and because of their intimacy, Jesus described God as one, not two or three.

HIS NATURE

We can know about God from the way that He has revealed Himself to mankind. We understand certain things to be true of God, even though there are some aspects of Him that remain a mystery. Still, we can understand His nature.

God is love, holy, and perfect, He is righteous and pure, and He does not change. He is the same "yesterday, today, and forever."[54] Because of His unchanging nature, He actively sustains the world,

---

[54]   Hebrews 13:8.

and we can depend on His blessings, for "every good gift and every perfect gift is from above,"[55] to sustain the life that He created on earth.

God has many characteristics, but His greatest attribute is love. To highlight this, the Scriptures state clearly in First John 4:8 that "he who does not love does not know God, for God is love." It is humbling to know that of all that He has created, God allowed His heart to be emotionally identified with humans to the extent that even though He is self-sufficient, He loves us and wants our love in return.

His love is personal and active, drawing us to Himself, and He does not just love us in some vague sense—rather, He has allowed His heart to be bound to us forever. The fact that He gave His only begotten Son to save us shows that when it comes to humans, His love knows no beginning and no end.

In the Bible, there are countless narratives that show God to be a great lover of people—especially people that cannot fight for themselves against tyranny and oppression—and even people that have been corrupted by sin are still protected and provided for and covered by His love.

HIS CHARACTER

In order to have an accurate understanding of the personality of God, it is wise to consult the Bible, because it has time and time again proven to be full of facts, undisputable evidence, and accurate knowledge regarding the origins of life, creation, and the Maker of all things. For example, the Scriptures reveal that the most important element of God's character is His holiness.

---

[55] James 1:17.

His holiness means that God is set apart and clearly separate from all that He created, and this is the foundation of all other aspects of His nature. It means that God is pure, cannot lie, and is honest, impartial, and fair. What He does is always right from a moral point of view. His holiness also means that God possesses a spiritual beauty that separates Him from all that is unclean and evil.

Because of this, Exodus 15:11 asks, "Who is like You, O LORD, among the gods? Who is like You, glorious in holiness, fearful in praises, doing wonders?" The holy nature of God portrays all His other attributes to show perfect balance and harmony, confirming the truth that there is no defect in God's character or His nature.

Commenting on this aspect of His nature, the Scriptures state in Revelation 4:11, "You are worthy, O Lord [Jehovah], to receive glory and honor and power; for You created all things, and by Your will they exist and were created."

God is good, and He wants good things for people and for the universe that He created. Further, the Bible tells us that He has personal knowledge of every person who has ever lived, those who are alive, and those who are yet conceived to be born, knowing them intimately in every way and providing life-giving sustenance for all of them. This is stated clearly in Jeremiah 1:5: "Before I formed you in the womb I knew you; before you were born I sanctified you [set you apart]."

He has given good things for us to enjoy, and He acts for the good of the entire universe according to His infinite knowledge and wisdom. On top of that, He showed us the utmost respect of granting us the free will to make the right choices, which differentiates us from all other creatures.

God is faithful and always keeps His promises. It is not surprising to know that because He originally created humans to have everlasting life, He sacrificed His precious Son, Jesus, to take the guilt of our sins away so we could regain salvation, benefit from His purposes, and become transformed as adopted sons of God.

He is also compassionate and moved by our sufferings and wants to help us. We may have been evil, but God is forgiving and merciful, and He does not bear grudges of past offenses, especially toward those who confess and forsake their sins and put their trust in Him.

But above all, God is a Father, a healer, a true protector, and a provider, who provides all things necessary for a joyful and meaningful life on earth. He knows what things you need before you even ask Him. That is why it should be a big relief for everyone to hear these encouraging words confirming what we are already assured of in Romans 8:38–39, which says:

For I am persuaded that neither death nor life, nor angels nor principalities nor powers, nor things present nor things to come, nor height nor depth, nor any other created thing, shall be able to separate us from the love of God which is in Christ Jesus our Lord.

On that note, I am compelled to say that the Bible couldn't have explained it any better.

GOD'S HANDWORK

In all of human history, every generation has been a witness to the fact that life comes from life and never from nonliving matter. This means that human life must originate from a very high and exceptionally intelligent living being, greater and higher than any other form of life. Therefore, everyone who has ever lived and walked on earth has been able to behold the evidence of the incredible and magnificent handwork of our glorious Creator.

Every day, billions of people all over the world are witnesses to the beautiful sunrises and sunsets, the faithfulness of the sun, the majestic clouds, the awesome brilliance of the moon, the orderly movements of the heavenly bodies, and the amazing design of living creatures. In fact, these examples are all the handwork of God, and they have been seen by all people at all times and in all places.

This prompted King David to declare in Psalm 19:1, "The heavens declare the glory of God; and the firmament [sky] shows His handiwork." And His work is seen not just in the heavens but when you consider the perfect intricacy of all living cells and the complexity of the amazing diversity of life on earth.

The glorious works of God can be seen in many different aspects of His creation, and for this reason, we must admit that we cannot fully understand God apart from His work, because all that He created reflects His character and flows from who He is, showing Him to be a scientific and artistic Master Craftsman who pays attention to detail and beauty.

If you pause for a moment to think about it, you will realize that the range and scale of what God created are truly staggering in a way that reveals His majesty and are indicative of His incomprehensible creativity and intelligence.

For example, the universe contains various objects of incredible sizes and masses at distances the human mind cannot fully grasp. To begin, let us consider the moon, which is a relatively small astronomical object, and yet, it is the nearest celestial piece of creation to the earth. It is approximately 3,400 kilometers in diameter and orbits at an average of 384,000 kilometers from the earth.

Even though this might seem to be a tremendous distance, it is noteworthy to mention that God has calculated with accurate precision to position the moon at the right distance from the earth to be of maximum benefit to the earth—a distance not too close and not too far.

It takes the moon one month to orbit the earth from start to finish in a roughly circular path, and this is how humans are able to formulate the idea of calculating the days for a "month." And from the Bible we know that one of the reasons God created the heavenly bodies was for them to be used for signs to mark the passage of time in knowing the days, the seasons, and the years, as explained in Genesis 1:14. Certainly, the moon does just that, because it continually travels round the earth every month with clockwork precision.

We must also remember that God designed the moon to rule over the night, as explained in Genesis 1:16–17. In fact, the moon outshines every other nighttime natural object, and it is worthy to note that when the moon is out—especially when it is at its full phase—it has the tendency to shine more than most astronomical objects, making them more difficult to see. It shines even far brighter than Venus, which is, next to the moon, earth's closest and brightest nighttime object in the universe.

As we keep looking farther outward into space, let us consider another example of what we understand from the Scriptures as the "greater light" created by God and designed by Him to rule over the day.

This celestial object is none other than the sun.

The sun is a star like no other because it is a glowing hot ball of hydrogen gas, which derives its energy from the fusion of hydrogen and helium at its core. It can be compared to an effective and stable hydrogen bomb that serves as an extremely efficient source of energy, positioned at the right distance to provide the correct amount of light and heat for the earth.

Scientists have discovered that the sun alone generates more energy every second than one billion major cities could produce in one year. If you think about the quantity of energy involved when God designed and created the sun, it might appear impossible to handle such an amount of energy, but because of His exceptional ingenuity, it is trivially easy for Him to develop and control such an immense phenomenon. However, it is beyond our human ability to fathom such an awesome intelligence used to achieve this.

Even though its presence is felt daily more than the moon, the sun is actually four hundred times more distant than the moon, and remarkably, it is also four hundred times larger than the moon. It is over one hundred times the size of the earth. This means it can contain more than one million earths, and it has a whopping distance of about 150 million kilometers from the earth.

This might seem incredible to humans, but just remember that it was not difficult at all for God to do this. It simply demonstrates His awesome power. That is why it is written in Jeremiah 32:17:

Ah, Lord GOD! Behold, you have made the heavens and the earth by Your great power and outstretched arm. There is nothing too hard for You.

When we think about the sun and the moon and all the other planets and how immense the universe truly is, we should certainly be impressed. But these are not the only things God has done, for He has even calculated and placed all of them with mathematical precision and unimaginable accuracy.

For instance, God also created our earth and placed it closer to the edge of our galaxy, which we refer to as the Milky Way. It is quite remarkable to know that even astronomers and scientists have concluded that our galaxy contains over 100 billion stars, and yet the Bible says in Isaiah 40:26 that God calls them all by their names. He also separated them far from each other. It is amazing to realize that God works on the grandest of scales, on a magnitude of unimaginable size.

It seems the more we contemplate all God has created, including the visible and invisible universe, the more it confirms that all of creation belongs to Him and proves beyond reasonable doubt that the creation of land, water, air, and the heavens out of nothing was miraculous. But even more spectacular is His creation of life.

It is astounding to know that God used His spoken word to bring various forms of life into existence. The Bible describes in Genesis 1:11–12 how it happened. It states, "Then God said, 'Let the earth bring forth grass, the herb that yields seed, and the fruit tree that yields fruit according to its kind, whose seed is in itself, on the earth'; and it was so. And the earth brought forth grass, the herb that yields seed according to its kind, and the tree that yields fruit, whose seed is in itself according to its kind. And God saw that it was good."

As we keep considering how He created life, the process reveals that God used every facet of His immense personality to bring things to life. And in order to make it simple for humans to understand, the Bible describes in fascinating detail how God said in Genesis 1:20–28, "'Let the waters abound with an abundance of living creatures, and let birds fly above the earth across the face of the firmament of the heavens.' So, God created great sea creatures and every living thing that moves, with which the waters abounded, according to their kind, and every winged bird according to its kind. And God saw that it was good. And God blessed them, saying, 'Be fruitful and multiply, and fill the waters in the seas, and let birds multiply on the earth.'"

But God was not done, for He is a Master Designer whose main desire is to create amazing and wonderful masterpieces on the grandest of scales on the largest canvas ever imagined into existence. This canvas, which He called earth, must be covered and filled in detail with the best of the very best of living creatures—from microorganisms to the largest of land and sea creatures.

Therefore, "God said, 'Let the earth bring forth the living creature according to its kind: cattle and creeping thing and beast of the earth, each according to its kind.' And it was so. And God made the beast of the earth according to its kind, cattle according to its kind, and everything that creeps on the earth according to its kind. And God saw that it was good."

How remarkable it is to note that after each of His creations, God paused, looked back to observe, and confirmed that it was good indeed according to His high standard of creative craftsmanship.

As we observe the handworks of God, we are continuously amazed to learn that the design and execution of all His creation projects are crafted and completed in a natural way full of beauty and balance, supported by abundant resources to provide protection and sustenance for His creatures.

Because of His outstanding nature of unparalleled goodness, He created a world filled with incredible diversity and variety, made up of different kinds of colors, tastes, sounds, scenery, animals, plants, and habitats. He decided to cap it all and sign off with His creation of humans in His own image, complete with intriguing varieties of size, color, and personality. In fact, He made everyone different in a way that there are no two persons completely alike, and He made sure we are each special in our own way.

The Bible assures us that God forms each one of us tenderly, lovingly, and intentionally and reinforces the fact that He wants us here. That is why, after creating the earth and other creatures before us, He created humans, male and female, in His own image. He blessed them and said to them, "Be fruitful and multiply; fill the earth and subdue it; have dominion over the fish of the sea, over the birds of the air, and over every living thing that moves on the earth."

Further, the Bible indicates that God went to great lengths to make sure that every one of us is unique in design and nature, and the physical body of humans is an amazing piece of engineering bearing testimony to this fact.

For instance, the human brain is so complex that scientists have barely begun to understand its intricacy, to the extent that no human being alive is making use of 100 percent of his brain capacity. The brain is not just complex, it is the perfect example of a well-organized and orderly arrangement of matter designed to handle billions of data.

However, as a whole, the most astounding of all creations is the human body. God designed it as a marvelous machine—capable, precise, and efficient—complete with a dynamic framework of bone and cartilage commonly referred to as the skeleton. The human skeleton is flexible, with hinges and joints designed to support, carry, and move the payload that makes up the physicality of the human figure. And to reduce harmful frictions, God showed His extraordinary attention to detail by making sure that the moving parts are lubricated. In order to achieve this objective, He installed an intricate chemical-refinery that produces, refines, lubricates, and replenishes blood and body fluids that run the entire system of our body.

This refinery-plant processes the food we eat into living tissue and causes the growth of flesh, blood, bones, and teeth. It converts the food we eat to generate energy for power, work, and for play, and it even repairs our body parts when they are damaged by accident or disease.

God also installed an advanced temperature-control system in our bodies with an automatic thermostat that regulates our bodies' heating and cooling systems, keeping our body temperature at about 37 degrees centigrade for maximum efficiency.

He designed the human eye to function in conjunction with the brain to help us see all the wonderful things around us in a manner ingenious and sophisticated and yet simple enough to operate on the basic principle that in our eye, the focus and aperture are adjusted automatically to function effectively in any environment.

God designed our ear and attached it at the perfect angles on our heads to ensure that sound waves are captured and transported down the auditory canal by sensitive bones of the middle ear to the cochlea, which is rolled up like a tiny seashell. He filled the cochlea with fluid so that it transforms airwaves to liquid, and He placed three tiny bones known as the ossicles precisely at the right spot next to them to translate the converted sounds so as to enable us to hear properly. Surprisingly, our Creator made sure that these little bones never grow along with our age, and their size does not change from the time we are born to the time we die.

The Creator designed the human heart as a muscular pump, with the average heartbeat of an adult beating at about sixty to one hundred beats per minute, pumping and forcing blood at this rate through hundreds of kilometers of blood vessels and transporting food nutrients and oxygen to every part of the body. It is awe inspiring to learn that the human heart pumps an average of six liters of blood every minute, and in one day, it pumps enough blood to fill more than forty drums of two-hundred-liter capacity.

Surely, the human body is a wonderful piece of engineering, and God used the basic raw materials found in the dust all over the world to prepare the basic chemicals He used in the right quantities to form and shape a human being. But the greatest rubber stamp of His ingenuity is portrayed in the way that He utilized these chemicals to form cell tissues, organs, nerves, and systems that circumnavigate the human body.

Finally, after creating this masterpiece He called man, God blew into his nostrils the breath of life, thereby adding an extra dimension to this creature that He had made in His own image and transformed him into a living soul with physical and spiritual capabilities. He made us this way to separate humans from animals, with the ability to pass on to the next generation this very same programmed information that is absolutely necessary to form another person, both physically and spiritually, in the original patent of His own image.

Therefore, the next time you observe another human being, please rest assured that what you see can only happen with the input of extraordinary and absolute intelligence, and he or she is a special and unique piece of creation and of immense value to our Creator. Certainly, it would not be an exaggeration to say that man is the masterpiece of God and the crown of His creation.

Many people before our present time have marveled at this creative aspect of God in the making of humans. It even prompted the psalmist in the Scriptures to declare in Psalm 139:14 (KJV):

> I will praise Thee; For I am fearfully and wonderfully made; marvelous are Thy works; and that my soul knoweth right well.

The extraordinary creations of God have answered all the questions regarding His personality and point the way forward, leading us to determine what His will is concerning His creation of the world and all that it contains. "His invisible attributes are clearly seen, being understood by the things that are made, even His eternal power and Godhead [divine nature]."[56]

Academically, there might be several interpretations challenging the story of creation, but none of them can successfully present evidence

---

[56] Romans 1:20.

to dispute the fact that the universe is the handiwork of a superior being whose intelligence is higher than anything on earth. This being is God the Creator, and for this reason, it would be foolish for anyone to say there is no God. Therefore, the worst kind of ignorance is the ignorance of not knowing who God really is.

CHAPTER FIFTEEN

WHAT IS THE REAL NAME OF GOD?

To know God is to discover the most beautiful, the most reliable, and the most rewarding reality there is. But to call upon His name is the greatest power readily available to each and every one of us, for no power is comparable to the power summoned by pronouncing the name of Almighty God.

But how can you summon real power through the name of God if you don't know His name—especially if you have heard many people call Him different names and wondered which one among the many names is the correct name of God?

From the Bible, we know that God has a name for all that He created, and even humans are known by their personal names. If so, wouldn't it be reasonable and appropriate for God to have a name? Certainly, humans understand that having and using personal names are a vital part of human relationships. So, the question is, should it be different when it comes to calling upon Him and when it comes to our friendship with God?

Surely, God has a name, but He also has many titles, and many of these titles are given to Him by us. Some of the titles include Almighty,

Lord, Creator, and God, which turns out to be the most popular. Nevertheless, it is clear to see that none of these titles is the name of God, and certainly, "God" is not the real name of God.

Surely, the title "God" is an identifier of what is being worshipped or who is being worshipped, and it shows utmost power or the mightiness of the Mighty One deserving worship. Because of this, the term "God" is not only used by Christians to address God. Other religions use the title "God" to refer to the Creator of all things as well.

For example, there is Allah, the Muslim god; Krishna, the Hindu god; Thor, the Viking god; and Zeus, the Greek god; and many other gods. Even in the Scriptures, there are numerous references to other gods, but God's personal name is used about seven thousand times in the Bible.

For accurate knowledge and interpretation of the name of God, it is remarkable to read Exodus 6:3, the passage that says, "I appeared to Abraham, to Isaac, and to Jacob, as God Almighty, but by My name LORD [Jehovah] I was not known to them." The Bible narrative regarding these men shows that they had a special relationship with God to the extent that they had a covenant with Him, and they understood truly they were dealing with God Almighty. But He chose not to tell them His name.

Surprisingly, God chose to reveal His name to another man who also had a special relationship with Him. In Exodus 3:13–14, the Bible reveals that when Moses encountered God in the burning bush, "Moses said to God, 'Indeed, when I come to the children of Israel and say to them, "The God of your fathers has sent me to you," and they say to me, "What is His name?" what shall I say to them?' And God said to Moses, 'I AM WHO I AM.' And He said, 'Thus you shall say to the children of Israel, "I AM has sent me to you." From this Bible narrative it is clear God chose to reveal His name to Moses and the Israelites by interpreting His name. He told them that His name is who He is, and moreover, that He is eternally present, He has always been, and He will always be whatever He chooses to be in order to carry out His plans.

When God said "I AM" to Moses, He spoke His name in the Hebrew language of the Israelites that this verse was written in. But many translations of the Bible also contain God's personal name. Therefore, the best place to seek for direction in this matter is to look further into the Scripture itself.

Evidence from the Bible reveals that the real name of God is "YHWH," and these four letters make up His name in Hebrew. However, these four letters have been translated into the English language as "Jehovah." And to underscore that this is His real name, God says in Isaiah 42:8 (ASV), "I am Jehovah, that is My name."

For many centuries, "Jehovah" has been the translation of God's name into English, largely used by Christians all over the world. Despite that many Bible scholars prefer the spelling "Yahweh" in place of "YHWH," the name "Jehovah" is the correct English form of the name that is most widely recognized as the name of God.

The Bible reminds us that there is power in the name Jehovah, and the power in His name can help anyone achieve and overcome. In fact, the name of God will help you to experience how majestic He is and how deeply He loves you. There are numerous stories in the Bible of people who have called upon the name Jehovah and used it to make possible what seemed impossible at that time.

Remember that God used His name "I AM" to reveal Himself and perform wonders to Moses and the Israelites. He will also use it to reveal who He wants to be for you and your loved ones. He did it several thousands of years ago when His name was first revealed to mankind, and He is just as present today to show you who He is and what He can do for you.

In the Old Testament of the Bible, you will find many appropriate ways to invoke the name of God, and many of them reveal who God wants to be for you.

For example, you can call Him "Yahweh." This means the self-existent One. He has always existed and will always exist. You can rely on Him because He is the eternal source of strength. Here are other powerful names of God:

- Jehovah-Jireh, which means "The Lord will provide."
- Jehovah-Rapha, which means "The Lord who heals."
- Jehovah-Nissi, which means "The Lord is our banner"—that is, He wages war on our behalf as Conqueror.
- Elohim, which refers to our "Creator."
- Adonai, which means "Lord Master."
- El Shaddai, which means "All-sufficient One," my Supplier.
- Jah-Jehovah, which uses the short and long forms of "The Lord," associated with His strength.
- Jehovah-Shalom, which means, "The Lord is Peace." When circumstances are chaotic, He gives peace beyond understanding, and whenever there are storms in your life, hide in Him.

Please feel confident to call upon Jehovah, for there is power beyond all human powers to be unleashed when you call upon and believe in His name.

CHAPTER SIXTEEN

THE WILL OF JEHOVAH

The will of Jehovah is that everything He wishes or desires will be done on earth as it is done in heaven. To show the importance of this, Jesus taught us to pray for His kingdom to come such that just as His will is done in heaven, so it will be done on earth.

It is Jehovah's will that you come to know Him as a person, draw close to Him, love Him as He loves you, and serve Him with your whole heart. It is necessary that everyone does this because there are tremendous benefits attached to this condition. That is why it is written in Psalm 37:4, "Delight yourself also in the LORD, and He shall give you the desires of your heart."

I am obliged to confide in you that if you put the application of this advice to the test, you will realize that the benefits gained far outweigh the effort you must put in. Even Jesus Himself said, "Blessed are those who hear the word of God and keep it."[57] And if you don't know how or where to begin, you can use the Bible to develop your spiritual power of reason to help you learn of His will for you.

---

[57]   Luke 11:28.

Furthermore, you can read in Romans 12:1–2 and confirm for yourself this encouraging advice, which says, "I beseech you therefore, brethren, by the mercies of God, that you present your bodies a living sacrifice, holy, acceptable to God, which is your reasonable service. And do not be conformed to this world, but be transformed by the renewing of your mind, that you may prove to yourselves what is the good and acceptable and perfect will of God."

Most certainly, it is the will of our Heavenly Father, Jehovah, that every single individual will have accurate knowledge of Him and His purpose for creating the earth and creating humans to take care of the earth. Even though that purpose was derailed several thousands of years ago, Jehovah has promised to remake the earth to be what He created it to be according to His original plans and intentions.

He wants everyone to have a chance to partake of a new earth and new system of things that Jesus will introduce. The objective to make this a reality is so important that He sent His Son, Jesus, to come to the earth to inform us about it and show us how He will rule and what we must do to become citizens of this new world. And finally, Jesus offered His life willingly so that everyone could gain access to the new kingdom of God.

This offer by Jesus proves that God permitted His love for the world and the people He created to override justified righteousness, which demands that all humans be judged. He allowed His love for us to move Him to offer a way out for mankind to be saved from the coming wrath that will cleanse the world of all evil. So, through this universal amnesty, God found a way to bring mankind to Himself in peace and friendship, and Jesus opted to be the broker of that peace.

The Bible informs us in John 3:16 (KJV), "For God so loved the world, that He gave His only begotten Son, that whosoever believeth in Him should not perish, but have everlasting life." When I consider this act by God from a human point of view, I would say that while God has no weakness, if He were to have one, it would be His unconditional love for mankind. But there is no single atom of weakness to be found in God, for He allowed His Son to die for very strong reasons:

Jehovah our God is just and fair, and He does not want humans to continue suffering from the results of the terrible decision made by their forbearers. He wants people to come to accurate knowledge of Him and have a chance to have everlasting life and fulfill their role in a new world according to His original scheme of things. For this purpose, He allowed His Beloved Son to come to earth to bring us this good news, to teach us by example how to live, and to die as a sacrifice that paves the way for this new world.

And to confirm the forthcoming arrival of a new world, the Scripture says in Revelation 21:1–4:

Now I saw a new heaven and a new earth, for the first heaven and the first earth had passed away. Also there was no more sea. Then I, John, saw the holy city, New Jerusalem, coming down out of heaven from God, prepared as a bride adorned for her husband. And I heard a loud voice from heaven saying, "Behold, the tabernacle of God is with men, and He will dwell with them, and they shall be His people. God Himself will be with them and be their God. And God will wipe away every tear from their eyes; there shall be no more death, nor sorrow, nor crying. There shall be no more pain, for the former things have passed away."

Surely, the Bible is resolute and unwavering regarding this message, because this is the absolute will of God, and He inspired the Scriptures to be written in such a way—from Genesis to Revelation—that this purpose will never be lost in translation.

In the Bible, you will also find much evidence indicating that the will of God must be accomplished. And even the Apostle John described a symbolic vision of a great rebirth in Revelation 22:1–2, where he made a clear reference to seeing a new heaven and a new earth. In his vision, John says:

> And he showed me a pure river of water of life, clear as crystal, proceeding from the throne of God and of the Lamb. In the middle of its street, on either side of the river, was the tree of life, which bore twelve fruits, each tree yielding its fruit every month. The leaves of the tree were for the healing of the nations.

Without any doubt, this amazing vision of John connects to the very beginning of the Biblical narrative of what happened in the Garden of Eden in the book of Genesis that led to the derailment of God's plan for humans by the jealous Satan. However, through this vision revealed to John, Jehovah is linking up with the events of the past, way back to the Old Testament—to the first pages of Genesis.

With this connection to the past, it is of paramount importance never to forget that Jehovah promised us a new heaven and a new earth. So, this is a new Garden of Eden, which means a paradise of eternal life where the will of God will reign supreme.

And the tree of life seen in this vision will be yielding fruit consecutively and providing nourishment to all in the new world because its roots have direct access to the eternal river of life that flows from the real source—God Himself. And all the people will be working together to cultivate the garden as Adam and Eve were supposed to do according to God's original plan for mankind.

Therefore, the fulfillment of Jehovah's purpose will come through Jesus, and this will result in the restoration of humans to their place as co-rulers and caretakers of God's world, ready to work in perfection under Jesus to take creation to the next level. And in keeping with this promise, all of mankind should be looking forward to a new heaven and a new earth, where righteousness, perfection, and the peace of God will dwell.

God has repeatedly used prophecies and visions written down and explained correctly in the Bible to reveal to us His promise of a new world, where humans will realize everlasting life in good health. This means that we will continue to grow and develop physically, spiritually, and intellectually.

Humans will gradually reach perfection to the extent of using 100 percent of our brains. Bear in mind that even in our present corrupt system of things, some spiritual masters and gurus have figured out that it is possible to use the mind to heal the body, and some scientists know that the human body can regenerate and repair itself, because the gene responsible for this function is in the human DNA.

And this gene is still embedded in humans, only it barely functions and seems to be switched off and substituted with death because of our sinful lives. Death is the absolute reward for sin. When God removes sin and sinful conditions, this gene will switch on full blast to reverse this condition, and mankind will have everlasting life—or at the very least, live for a thousand years in the first millennium of Jesus Christ's rule, as described in the Bible in Revelation 20:1–6.

Just imagine what you can achieve in a state of perfection, what you can do with a perfect body, or what you can create with a perfect brain. If you are a musician, a scientist, or an inventor, then you will be operating on a level higher than that of a genius. Maybe you are an athlete, footballer, or a sportsperson—then you will become what is now regarded as a super athlete, or even better.

Just imagine what this will mean to humanity. Imagine how you will feel to see your loved ones again who passed away many years ago, or to hear directly from people like Abraham, Isaac, Jacob, Moses, David, Solomon, Peter, and Paul—or even somebody like William Tyndale, who was persecuted and burnt alive because he translated the Bible so everyone could read and understand it. Yes, this is not a fantasy; it is a reality, because the Bible tells us that they will hear His voice and come out.[58]

It is noteworthy to remember that this will not be the first time for resurrection, because when Jesus resurrected Lazarus and the young girl in the New Testament, they were reunited with their families and friends here on earth. And this will also happen in the future in a much better environment and on a larger scale, because those who are brought back to life on earth will have the opportunity to live forever and never die again. Moreover, they will live in a perfect world different from the one we live in today, with no war, no crime, and no sickness.

---

[58]   John 5:25–29.

Assuredly, the Bible confirms in Revelation 20:13, "The sea gave up the dead who were in it, and Death and Hades delivered up the dead who were in them." This shows that billions of people will live again. Bear in mind that this is not impossible, for Jesus has already shown His ability to wake people up from death. Nonetheless, the Bible earlier informed us that; "Eye has not seen, nor ear heard, nor have entered into the heart of man the things which God [Jehovah] has prepared for those who love Him."[59] Certainly, wonderful and amazing surprises await all in the new world.

All we need to do to live in the coming kingdom of God is to change our crooked and sinful ways and focus on things that reflect the image of God to show that we believe in His power to save us and appreciate this great change that will happen on our behalf. In fact, it would be an understatement to conclude that it is an exciting prospect to know that we can have an everlasting wonderful life on earth in the not-so-distant future.

With this exhilarating good news, just imagine the kind of good times that humans will be able to enjoy in the new world. When I think of the possibilities for humans, I get super excited, and so should you. Therefore, it would be a total misconception to think that in the new world, it will only be about praise, prayer, and worship, for even in heaven the angels are known to rejoice and celebrate and sing joyful songs of happiness, and our Heavenly Father is known to be a happy God.

This is the true meaning of what the Scriptures are all about from Genesis to Revelation. For this main purpose, Jehovah inspired men

---

[59]   First Corinthians 2:9.

to write the Bible to inform mankind of His promise to bring His well-planned intentions for humans to a successful completion. This is the summary of the comprehensive message of the Bible, and it is of paramount importance that everyone gets to hear this good news and understand fully what it means.

The rest of the information in the Bible contains the detailed essential elements of human existence from the beginning. A diverse spectrum of valuable instructions on any subject or situation, and examples to help humans live happy, successful, prosperous, and meaningful lives with the hope of this wonderful everlasting life promised to us by God. For, God understands that without hope there is no life—everything else is meaningless.

And, for this reason, I encourage everyone to have hope and show faith and know that Jehovah has planned ahead already and put mechanisms in place that introduce continuity into His creation for a purpose. That is why He divided twenty-four hours into night and day—so that one will usher in the other. So, tomorrow is the hope of today, just as today becomes the hope of yesterday, and everlasting life in absolute perfection is the real hope for every human being—not power, riches, fame, or glory, for all they represent is vanity.

OUR LORD'S PRAYER

Now that we know what the will of God for us is, we need no longer be apprehensive of the coming kingdom of God or be fearful of the manner in which it will be achieved—whether it happens via the battle of Armageddon, as revealed in Revelation 16:16, or through any means that Jesus deems appropriate to establish His theocratic reign. Rather, we should keep on praying for its imminent arrival.

And for this purpose, it would be most suitable to pray like Jesus taught us to do, for He understands that Jehovah's will is the best for mankind:

Therefore, let us pray:

> Our Father which art in heaven, hallowed be Thy name. Thy kingdom come, Thy will be done on earth, as it is in heaven.
> Give us this day our daily bread.
> And forgive us our debts, as we forgive our debtors.
> And lead us not into temptation, but deliver us from evil.
> Amen.[60]

---

[60] Matthew 6:9–13 KJV.

SYNOPSIS

This book explores the reason why the earth is continually debased by human errors-intentional and unintentional. It provides a comprehensive insight into what must be done to return it to a harmonious place for all of humanity as it was supposed to be.

It is full of surprises that will encourage anyone to seek for solutions like millions of people who are now asking the most puzzling questions about current news headlines all over the globe—on wars, environmental issues, corruption, global recession, hunger, crime and pandemics. Including the vast majority who are wondering why it looks as if anything that can go wrong is about to go wrong.

Suppose you could find answers to these complicated issues. Answers that provide astounding truths and profound logic that will help you to make sense of it all. It explains how anyone can develop resilience to overcome the challenges of the present system of things. In The King of Kings, you will find the key to a new way of living in a long-lasting relationship with God.